NON-RENUNCIATION

Themes and Interpretations of Hindu Culture

NON-RENUNCIATION

Themes and Interpretations of Hindu Culture

T. N. MADAN

DELHI
OXFORD UNIVERSITY PRESS
NEW YORK OXFORD
1987

Oxford University Press, Walton Street, Oxford OX2 6DP

NEW YORK TORONTO
DELHI BOMBAY CALCUTTA MADRAS KARACHI
PETALING JAYA SINGAPORE HONG KONG TOKYO
NAIROBI DAR ES SALAAM
MELBOURNE AUCKLAND
and associates in
BEIRUT BERLIN IBADAN NICOSIA

Printed in India by P. K. Ghosh
at Eastend Printers, 3 Dr Suresh Sarkar Road, Calcutta 700014
and published by R. Dayal, Oxford University Press
YMCA Library Building, Jai Singh Road, New Delhi 110001

For

UMA, VIBHAS, and VANDANA

ihalokaḥ eva paralokaḥ

CONTENTS

PREFACE

This book has been written over a period of almost ten years. In fact, the idea that a book was taking shape dawned on me only a couple of years ago when all but one chapter and the Introduction were already in print or typescript. In preparing the present version of the various chapters the revisions have ranged from minor corrections and alterations to extensive rewriting. I have not, however, eliminated entirely the overlapping of the chapters. While this has resulted in some looseness of construction, it has the advantage of making it convenient for the reader to read the book not only as it ideally should be, from cover to cover, but also piecemeal, chapter by chapter. I should, however, emphasize that the theme of the book—it has one: *the worthwhileness of the life of the man-in-the-world*—and my attempt to provide interpretations of it will become clear only if all of it is read and in the sequence in which the chapters are laid out. Since I have written of the theme and the interpretations at some length in the Introduction, I will not elaborate this point any further.

T. N. MADAN

Delhi
12 September 1985

ACKNOWLEDGEMENTS

I am obliged to the editors and publishers of various books and journals for their permission to include in this book materials published by them earlier in more or less the same form. Chapters 1, 2 and 3 respectively appeared originally in *Contributions to Indian Sociology* (Institute of Economic Growth, Delhi, 1981), *Purity and auspiciousness*, edited by John B. Carman and Frédérique A. Marglin (E. J. Brill, Leiden, 1985), and *Culture and morality*, edited by Adrian C. Mayer (Oxford University Press, Delhi, 1981). The Epilogue is based on an essay of the same title published in *International Social Science Journal* (Unesco, Paris, 1977) and a lecture (now under publication) delivered at Marlboro College (USA) in 1984. An earlier draft of Chapter 5 was presented to a seminar on 'Order and anomie', organized by the Social Science Research Council, New York, in New Delhi in 1982. I am grateful to the Council and to its Research Associate, David Szanton, for the invitation to write the paper and for their subsequent consent to making my own arrangement for publication. Besides Chapter 5, Chapter 4 and the Introduction are being published here for the first time.

I owe a deep debt of gratitude to the following friends and colleagues for reading one or more chapters and giving me their advice: John Barnes, Brenda Beck, G. S. Bhatt, John Carman, Veena Das, Louis Dumont, Shrivatsa Goswami, Ron Inden, R. S. Khare, Bh. Krishnamurthy, F. K. Lehman, Frédérique Marglin, Ashis Nandy, Jonathan Parry, A. K. Ramanujan, Kanti Shah, Baidyanath Saraswati, Kailas Sharma, M. N. Srinivas, Meenakshi Thapan, and Jit Singh Uberoi.

I am additionally indebted to Kris Lehman for suggesting the title of the book.

I should not forget to mention here the anthropology and religion students of Harvard University who heard this book in the form of lectures (under the title of 'Perplexities in everyday life') during the Fall Term of 1984 in John Carman's class on Hindu ethics. Their keen interest and John Carman's gentle questioning are responsible in no small way for encouraging me to get the book ready for publication. I am grateful to all of them.

I must place on record once again my indebtedness to the Institute of Economic Growth, Delhi, where I have had the freedom to pursue my studies in directions chosen by myself and where this book was written.

Finally, I must thank the Oxford University Press for their confidence in the prospects for this book.

A NOTE ON TRANSLITERATION

Well-established conventions have been followed in rendering Sanskrit and Hindi words in Roman. Long vowels are shown thus: ā (आ) as in father, ī (ई) as in machine, ū (ऊ) as in rule.

Among consonants, attention may be drawn to the following : g (ग) as in goat, ṅ (ङ) as in ink, c (च) as in church, ñ (ञ) as in Spanish señor, ś (श) as in sugar, ṣ (ष) as in shun. Besides, there is the distinction between cerebral and dental consonants: t (त), th (थ), d (द), dh (ध), n (न), and ṭ (ट), ṭh (ठ), ḍ (ड), ḍh (ढ), ṇ (ण). S (स) as in sun is also a dental consonant. Aspirated consonants have the letter h added to them: kh (ख), gh (घ), ch (छ), jh (झ), th (थ), dh (ध), ṭh (ठ) ḍh (ढ), ph (फ), bh (भ).

The use of ṁ nasalizes the preceding vowel (as in *saṁskāra*) and ḥ indicates a preceding breathing vowel (as in *śatruḥ*).

Kashmiri words (in Chapters 1, 2 and 5) pose special problems. For simplicity and comparability, original Sanskrit words have been used whenever it has been possible to trace these from their spoken Kashmiri form.

All common nouns from Sanskrit and other Indian languages which are not to be found in the *Oxford English Dictionary* have been italicized and provided with diacritical marks. Personal and place names, names of rivers and mythological figures, and the titles of traditional 'texts' have been printed in Roman without diacritical marks, which have been, however, added to them in the Index. Titles of authored texts (ancient as well as modern) have been italicized without diacritical marks, which are, again, provided in the Index.

INTRODUCTION
INTIMATIONS OF THE GOOD LIFE

The better trained we are
The more we doubt ourselves.
KALIDASA

It is not permitted to know all things.
HORACE

And what you do not know is the only thing you know.
T. S. ELIOT

SCOPE, DATA, METHODS

Much has been written about the salience of *sannyāsa,* or renunciation, in Hindu culture. The theme of this book, however, is non-renunciation as a value. And it is a book of interpretations.

Hindu society is best known by caste, its most characteristic institution, and by renunciation, perhaps its best-known cultural ideal. The interpretation offered in this book is that, although renunciation is undoubtedly a remarkable value orientation which permeates the world-view of even the worldly householder, it does not bestow its distinctive character upon the everyday life of Hindus. Caste and renunciation are in fact antithetical though complementary[1]: while the former, based on a logic of difference and solidarity, provides a broad social framework for individual and group action in a world of social relations, the latter is its repudiation as both value and empirical condition. What is in consonance with caste is domesticity with its values of auspiciousness, purity and moral equipoise.

Renunciation has been traditionally regarded not as an arbi-

[1] Depending on one's perspective, either of these relations may be stressed. Thus, Dumont places the emphasis on complementarity: 'It may be doubted whether the caste system could have existed and endured independently of its contradictory, renunciation' (1980: 186).

trary annulment of the life of the man-in-the-world but, and in fact ideally, as its culmination. Such a viewpoint may be derived from the Manusmriti itself, perhaps the best-known of the *dharmaśāstra* texts, which forbids men to become renouncers until they have discharged the traditional three debts (to gods, gurus and ancestors) by living the life of the householder. Kane in his monumental survey of the *dharmaśāstra* concludes that the overall tendency 'is to glorify the status of an householder and push into the background the two *āśramas* of *vānaprastha* and *sannyāsa*, so much so that certain works say that these are forbidden in the Kali age' (1941: 424). In fact, Kane points out, some prominent *dharmaśāstra* writers such as Gautama and Baudhayana looked upon the stage of the householder as the only stage of life (ibid.: 640).

And yet, renunciation has been considered the supreme value among the Brahmans who were the ideologues of Hindu society. Thus, it has been asserted that the social pre-eminence of the Brahman is based not on his 'monopoly of Vedic knowledge', or on his priesthood, but 'on his being the exponent of the values of renunciation' (Heesterman 1985: 44). More generally, renunciation has been called by Dumont 'a sort of universal language of India' (1970: 52), and the renouncer has been identified by him as 'the creator of values' in Indian religion and philosophy (ibid.: 46). Indeed, Dumont maintains, 'what one is in the habit of calling Indian thought is for the very great part the thought of the sannyasi' (ibid.: 12). No wonder, then, that the Hindu has been seen all over the world in the image of the sannyasi: a truly magnificent, even theatrical, figure who gives away all his possessions, performs his own mortuary rites to proclaim the severance of all human bonds, and lives a highly disciplined life of austerities—a homeless wanderer, 'an emaciated figure . . . with his begging bowl, his staff and orange dress' (ibid.: 44).

Though he may be tall and splendid, the renouncer is by no means the only actor on the Hindu stage of life. In fact he is not on the stage at all, having left it, but looks at it from the sidelines, as it were. The figure in the centre of the stage is a rather homely character, namely, the householder (*gṛhastha*). If not exactly cast in a heroic mould, he is not the 'phantom-like' man either that Dumont (1970: 48) considers him to be.

It is the ideal of his life to 'live in the world' but to do so in the light of the renouncer's philosophy (see Dumont, 1970: 12, 41 *et passim*). Translated into the householder's idiom, renunciation becomes the twin ideals of self-possession and detachment in the midst of worldly involvements which are not considered by him evil in themselves. What he seeks to resist is being enslaved by such involvements. He hopes to mediate between total indulgence and total renunciation. It is, indeed, all a matter of relations.

This book is, then, about the householder, about his affirmation of a disciplined this-worldly life as the good life. The chapters comprising it, each complete in itself, contribute to the elaboration of the main theme. I begin with a discussion of the ideology of the householder in which the purposes and procedures of the good life, lived in affirmation of the values of plenitude and detachment, are spelled out (Chapter 1). The householder's way of life is further examined in the light of the fundamental values of auspiciousness and purity (Chapter 2). It is shown to be marked by the endeavour to establish a balance between, and, in fact, overcome the trap of, binary opposites such as asceticism and eroticism (Chapter 3). It acknowledges the sovereignty of good: the desired must be brought under the regime of, and encompassed by, the preferred (Chapter 4). And the final testimony of the good life is the good death which one endeavours to attain without fear (Chapter 5). All this is what the tradition says: but definitions of the good life change, new values emerge, causing perplexities. Thus, the modern Indian is invited by the world around him to define his life in terms of the ideologies of secularism, development and democracy which have been diffused from the West. The translation of cultural traditions from one into another is, however, always problematic and the modern Hindu suffers from the strain of a fragmented consciousness. It is with a statement of this predicament that the book ends (Epilogue).

The data on which the book is based are derived from three main sources: first, my own intensive fieldwork among the Brahmans of the Kashmir Valley (Chapters 1, 2 and 5) and more general inquiries among some Brahman communities of Uttar Pradesh (Chapter 2); second, written ethnographic accounts, mostly published, of some Hindu (or Hinduized) communities of Uttar Pradesh, Orissa and Karnataka (Chapter 2); and third, contemporary works of fiction dealing with ancient and contemporary times in Bihar, north India, Karnataka and Tamilnadu (Chapters 3 and 4). Some historical and sociological works have been consulted to present the modern quest for Hinduism (Epilogue).

Though the data used in this book are mainly about Brahmans, the cultural themes they illustrate are, I think, of much wider import. It is, of course, well known that cultural diversity within Hindu society, in terms of inter-regional and inter-caste differences (not to bring in the dimension of diachrony), is so great that every general statement about it is suspect—that the sociology of Hindu society can at best be an exercise in suspicion—and that the more trained we are the more likely it is that we will ourselves doubt what we write or say. While the need for caution could hardly be over-stressed, I do not think we should allow ourselves to be dazzled by ethnographic diversity into a condition of sightlessness.

We must ceaselessly endeavour to look beyond the enormous variety of cultural forms for some major themes or 'dynamic affirmations' which are the 'key' to their 'character, structure and direction',[2] and which through mutual reinforcement or mutual limitation bestow on all of them a civilizational distinctiveness. These themes, it may be expected, will find more elaborate articulation in the world-views of certain Hindu castes and communities with their long literary traditions, which in the main link them to one another, than of others, but they are of general applicability. This is true above all of the high value placed on the life of the householder, which is what the good life means, and has always meant, to most Hindus irrespective of differences of caste, sect or region. What is more, in all matters involving the performance of rituals under the direction of Brahman priests, the values, beliefs and customs of the Brahmans themselves have spread to other castes and communities, producing a palpable cohesiveness among Hindus (see Srinivas 1967). This book is thus about Hindu society, though

[2] I have employed here some words and phrases from a long-forgotten paper by Morris Opler. I should hasten to add, though, that my use of the word 'theme' does not follow Opler's closely (see Opler 1945).

the thematic perspectives offered are first and foremost of the Brahmans.

Turning from the scope of the book to the data on which it is based: the use of data generated through my own inquiries and of published ethnographic and historical works has posed no more than the usual problems for me. I have taken a risk, however, in consciously moving away from the beaten tracks and choosing to treat novelists with respect as highly motivated informants, and novels as first or second order interpretations of socio-cultural reality which provide invaluable insights into the moral perplexities that a people experience. Such interpretations themselves have to be interpreted, however, to supplement and stimulate ethnography.

Anticipating scepticism on the part of some colleagues, I had clarified briefly the justification for my reliance upon works of fiction in the essay that appears as Chapter 3 in this book. I had referred to the novels chosen as the basis of my discussion as 'fragments of the original discourse of contemporary Hindu intellectuals'. Further, I had pointed out that, if a novel appeals to a wide variety of readers, it must tell us something that is of deep and general concern in their society: its significance is made manifest through a shared grammar of response. I might, however, add a few words of elucidation.

Now, the fundamental question raised in the novels I have chosen for discussion is about the struggle of the individual, considered as a moral agent, to grapple with the contrary and powerful pulls of asceticism and eroticism (see Chapter 3). This struggle is one of the abiding themes of Hindu classical literature, as it is of living folklore. It is also the very stuff of everyday life. Is there a Hindu villager, illiterate and unsophisticated though he may be, who is not familiar with the debauchee and the ascetic, with the life of sensuality as opposed to that of spirituality? Similarly (turning to the other chapter, in this book, based on a novel), are extra-marital love and illegitimacy not moral problems faced by every village community in India one time or another? It is true that extant ethnographic accounts are usually silent on these issues; but even ethnographers know how significant these moral problems are in the so-called real life.

It may be argued that such predicaments are present, but that the kind of moral discourse found in novels is unfamiliar; this really depends upon who one is talking with. Not only is the social distribution of knowledge within a community uneven, but its expression, too, is multivocal. The so-called common people have access to the same sources of tradition as the literati, though the channels of communication are different and there are, therefore, differences in the form of the messages that they exchange among themselves.

The characteristically Platonic dichotomy between cognition and creative imagination has persisted to the present day, but it did not prevent Karl Marx or Sigmund Freud from deriving inspiration from literature. While the former referred to Prometheus as the foremost saint and martyr in the philosopher's calendar, the latter—Freud of course considered himself very much a scientist—confessed that wherever he went he found a poet had been there before him. More recently, Erving Goffman (1961), David Plath (1980) and others have by their brilliant use of incidents and characters from novels shown the immense scope of illuminations that the novel affords to the social scientist. Rather than elaborate further, I will only say that I find the distinction between 'real' and 'imagined' worlds, when pressed too far, unduly limiting (see Berger 1977).

A few words about my approach to the elucidation of the selected themes are now in order. To put it simply, my method is ethnographic, that is, it is descriptive and interpretive and based on the assumption that it is culture-laden, or meaningful social relations which are our primary concern: individuals and events interest us only derivatively (that is, relationally). Reflecting upon the data at my disposal, I seek to present interpretations of certain crucial relationships (husband and wife, parent and child), events (death), predicaments or moral dilemmas (extra-marital love, annunciation or renunciation of the householder's life, modernization), and values (auspiciousness, purity, selflessness, fidelity, piety). I use the word interpretation with some hesitation for fear that it is currently fashionable in some scholarly circles but, given the prevailing paradigmatic factionalism in social-cultural anthropology, it raises serious misgivings in others. I should therefore explain my position in a little more detail.

As I write in Chapter 1, I am not searching for explanations of human behaviour in terms of causes or determinants, though I do not deny that human actions may be seen to have material causes, practical ends and concrete consequences. I know that 'love' has been characterized as the 'independent variable' in the Bengali Hindu kinship system (see Inden and Nicholas 1977: 88), but that is not what my approach is to the study of culture. My focus is not on causal chains but on subjective meanings. I have tried to understand and explicate some commonsense notions, as also some relatively refined categories of thought in terms of which Hindus make sense of their everyday life to themselves. They do so through the piecing together or connecting of ideas and actions, of memories of the past, predicaments of the present, and hopes or visions of the future, and this too is interpretation. But while the interpretations fabricated by the people themselves may seem adequate and explicit to them, they may yet be opaque to the outsider, which is what the social anthropologist usually is, in one sense or another: if not born in another society, his training as an anthropologist teaches him to turn a sceptical eye at everything that seems familiar. In other words, depending upon who he is, he either seeks to live intimately with strangers or acts the stranger among intimates.

I agree with those students of human cultures, such as Clifford Geertz, who deny that anthropologists have any special gifts for empathy and powers of imagination. The people's interpretations are, therefore, our data, just as what we hear and see are our data. They are the principles, as Louis Dumont might say, in terms of which we are able to make sense of what is heard or seen and, as such, they belong to a higher level than the other data. In other words, our informants are not just informers, they are also interpreters, but their perspectives on everyday life may not always converge. The commentaries of the Hindu householder and the renouncer on life in the world will surely not be the same.

Interpretation thus involves the social anthropologist in a process of unfolding or unravelling what are at first riddles to him, by working out their implications. It is not only the idea with which we set out that gets explicated through this process, but also its collateral or opposite, its principle of control. We move from simplicity to complexity and hope 'to formulate clearly what one has more or less confusedly perceived' (Dumont 1970: 36). This mode of interpretation consists of observation of the flux of everyday life and a turning away from it to seek the sources of its stability; it involves believing the people and disbelieving them too; it entails the connecting of the concrete with the abstract—in short, it is a search with the critical eye and ear for significance and structure.

Just as the internal interpreters are several, the external interpreters also may be many, each capturing a particular facet of social reality—visualizing it as a system, a structure, a stratagem, a text, consciousness, or whatever—and providing a perspective on it. To say this is not to surrencer to nihilism, but to affirm the legitimacy and value of pluralism. I will not, however, go so far as to suggest that the birth of the interpreters of action may be seen to signal the death of the authors of action. I claim no more than having raised some basic questions about the constitution of the good life in Hindu society and to have provided some intimations about how they may be answered in terms of the conceptual categories of the people. In the final reckoning, I know that the people among whom I have done fieldwork, or about whom I have read, know much more about themselves than I ever will, though I may know things about them that they themselves do not. Indeed, as Horace told us long ago, we are not permitted to know all things. The illusions of completeness or permanence that an ethnographic text creates are useful and partake of the truth, but they are, nevertheless, illusions. The interpretive endeavour knows no finality—which does not mean that it is uninterested in theoretical conclusions—but only turnings and pauses and understandings and, then, new turnings. Each understanding is a preface to yet another, each 'arrival' a 'point of departure'. As the questions change, so do the answers, and the completeness of description is inevitably deferred. I believe the positivists of yesteryear knew this as well as the grammatologists of today. The aims and the nature of the endeavour are, however, clear: namely, the effort to make sense of what the people we seek to understand think and do, and as Max Weber puts it, to grasp how they 'confer meaning and significance' on their lives. Our interpretations are thus not pictures of empirical reality, and intentionally so. They are descriptive but they are not merely description. We do not only *look* and *listen*, we also *think*.

THE THEMES

I should now like to introduce the various themes discussed in this book under the broad rubric of *the good life*. The opening chapter, 'Domesticity and Detachment', was originally presented at a conference on the Indian concepts of person held at Harvard in 1976, and later published in that form (see Madan 1983). A revised version had already been published earlier (see Madan 1981b), and the interpretation offered in the two versions was the same. The text used here is that of the 1981 version, with some minor alterations.

It may be pointed out that, though my discussion of the ideology of the householder is based on my studies of the Brahmans of the Kashmir Valley, there is, as already stated, ample evidence in indological and ethnographical literatures of the life of the householder being the most highly valued in Hindu society. To present but one more piece of evidence here, we find that many of the major protestant sectarian movements of medieval times, which count their followers in millions today, emphasized the virtues of disciplined domesticity as against renunciation. Basava (*c.* 1125–1270?), the founder of the Lingayat sect in the south, Nanak (1469–1538), the first of the Sikh gurus in the north, Vallabha (1479–1531), the promulgator of the *puṣṭi mārga* (way of abundance) in the west, and Chaitanya (1485–1534), founder of a popular sect in the east based on an exultation in divine and conjugal love, extolled domesticity as the good life as long as it was an affirmation of the bliss of the union of the devotee and the deity, and not a contradiction of it.

While the Lingayat and the Sikh faiths steadfastly upheld the value of domesticity and the sanctity of conjugal love, some of the other sects did slide occasionally into eroticism without formally abandoning the domestic ideal. As pointed out earlier in this Introduction, the *dharmaśāstra* literature, and, in fact, the epics also, are highly eulogistic of the householder's state. In view of such evidence, it seems legitimate to suggest that an ideology of the householder exists in Hindu society. The householders are not merely given empirically, in defiance of the ideology of renunciation, but domesticity is also a positive value orientation, just as renunciation is. This raises the important question of the relationship between two apparently antithetical ideologies.

It is obvious that the two ideologies cannot prevail at the same level. A hierarchical view is, therefore, imperative. If we maintain that, though renunciation is not normal (in the sense of not being common), and is yet the most highly idealized state, the values then expressed through renunciation are all-encompassing: the householder may, obviously, live only in the shadow of the renouncer, and, if not merging in him, be certainly guided by him. This, indeed, would seem to be the implication of the emphasis upon detachment (*virakti*) laid by the Kashmiri Brahmans I have studied and doubtless by millions of tradition-oriented Hindus. But, as Dumont puts it (in another context), 'the moment [a] second function is defined, it entails reversals for the situations belonging to it' (1982: 225). The hostility towards renouncers, which is paradoxically combined with reverence for them among householders (and of which I write in Chapter 1), would seem to point to the vulnerability, if not also the inauthenticity, of the choice of renunciation if it flows from a sense of defeat rather than of fulfilment. It is only when one has fulfilled the obligations of householdership, and also enjoyed them, that one may experience desirelessness, which is the essential condition of renunciation. The paradox disappears: the repudiation of renunciation by the householder does not affect its validity as a value at the higher level.

The householder, I suggest, hears, day after day, the knock on his front door of the sannyasi, who literally stands there asking for alms, and suggesting a future (even instant) possibility, and the knock of the *bhogī* (enjoyer, sensualist) on his back door, as it were, who invites him to a life of unbridled pleasure. The value of his state of householdership is challenged and threatened by both. His success would seem to lie in his ability to resist complete surrender to either and combine the principles of domesticity (*gārhasthya*) and detachment (*virakti*).

Domesticity for the Hindu is inseparable from a feeling of

well-being and happiness, embodying the values of auspiciousness and purity—the theme of the second chapter. It is reproduced here without any major change from the volume (see Carman and Marglin 1985) which resulted from a conference on auspiciousness and purity held in 1980 at George Washington University, Washington, D.C., under the auspices of the Conference on Religion in South India. It is an exploratory essay and suggests a line of inquiry for elucidating the significance of the relatively neglected notion of auspiciousness (*śubha*) in relation to the much studied notion of purity (*śuddha*), namely, to examine it as referring essentially to the significance of temporal events in human lives. As a pervasive value in domestic life, auspiciousness is not confined to upper caste Hindus, though it is a more important motif in their households. All over India, one sees graphic representations of auspiciousness in the form of geometric or floral patterns (made with white lime powder, yellow turmeric powder, red brick dust, etc., or with pastes of them) on the façades of homes and on the ground in front of them. I have seen these signs of auspiciousness in the huts of the poorest, low caste, illiterate villagers as well as in the homes of the rich upper castes. These graphic representations, almost invariably made by women (suggesting a special relationship between auspiciousness and femininity), are derived from *maṇḍala* and *yantra*, which are abstract depictions of an orderly cosmos.

I have read a number of important discussions of auspiciousness, or of other themes that include discussions of it, in the last five years since I wrote my own essay—by, among others, Veena Das, Frédérique Marglin and Vasudha Narayanan. Some of them seem to reinforce the approach suggested by me, while others have extended their inquiries in related ways. Thus, Das (1982: 143ff) rightly seeks to construct a unified paradigm of auspiciousness and inauspiciousness, purity and pollution, and life and death. That her commendable effort needs both qualification and clarification only underscores the complexity of the task in hand. For example, she does not allow of the possibility of thinking of death as auspicious in certain circumstances (see Narayanan 1985 and Chapter 5 below). Marglin thinks that it is 'premature to restrict the meaning of those terms which are translated as auspiciousness to the passage of time' (1985: 293). She is perhaps right, perhaps not.[3] What is important is that the notion of auspiciousness is being increasingly recognized as an important subject requiring careful study.

I am convinced that the well-established emphasis on the study of purity/impurity, though undoubtedly of fundamental importance in the study of Hindu society, does not provide by itself a sufficiently adequate framework of values for the study of domestic life. This realization dawned upon me many years ago in the course of my study of family life among the Kashmiri Brahmans, who are, therefore, my first teachers on this subject. It seems to me that a unified theory of auspiciousness and purity would provide yet another link between caste and the family in the domain of values, that is, in terms of the notion of the good life. Auspiciousness/inauspiciousness is also a feature of intercaste relations as I point out in passing in my discussion (Chapter 2 below).[4]

Chapter 3, 'Asceticism and Eroticism', originally written in 1978 and published three years later (see Madan 1981a), is reproduced here with some minor changes. In it I develop further the notion of the tension of the two extremes of asceticism (*tapas*) and eroticism (*kāmuktā*) which the life of the householder, as discussed in Chapter 1, seeks to overcome. This is, of course, one of the fundamental moral dilemmas treated for very long in Hindu literary, philosophical and mythological traditions. The renouncer and the enjoyer are both towering personalities; the one proclaims self-control (*ātma-niyantraṇa*), and the other proclaims the power of enjoyment (*bhoga*). The king is the ideal enjoyer (*bhoktṛ*). But, it is argued in this chapter, the life of enjoyment, when apotheosized, leads to perdition, just as renunciation may turn out to be an empty gesture of self-mortification.

[3] The word Marglin herself cites most often in the context of auspiciousness is *maṅgala* It is of interest to note that some lexicographers have derived *maṅgala* from *maṅg* which indicates movement—in first person, to move, to go.

[4] It may be noted that in this as also in Chapters 2 and 5 I have focused on certain key verbal symbols because it seems to me that people's perception of the situations they find themselves in and, therefore, their manner of relating to them, are shaped significantly by lexical categories. I do not, however, want to commit myself to this methodological position dogmatically at the cost of underestimating the importance of grammar.

All this is well known. The point I want to stress here is that the *ideal* Hindu solution to this moral dilemma is not a simple harmonization of opposites, though many knowledgeable scholars seem to think so. Thus, an otherwise fascinating recent study of passion and renunciation in Hindu culture characterizes the 'harmonization of contrary impulses . . . as a recurrent theme in Indian culture and as an issue which is at once intimately personal and mysteriously universal' (Siegel 1983: xi). The moral perplexity of the Hindu is, indeed, 'intimately personal' and 'mysteriously universal', but his *ideal* by way of a response to it is the cultivation of a moral sensibility which carries one beyond having to make moral choices and coerce oneself into a particular course of action. A widely influential contemporary Hindu philosopher, J. Krishnamurti, puts it thus: 'What is important, surely, is to be aware without choice, because choice brings about conflict. The chooser is in confusion, therefore he chooses; if he is not in confusion there is no choice' (Lutyens 1970: 70).[5] The good life is, then, above all a life of freedom from external controls: it is an inner state of maturation and grace.

Chapter 4 is a continuation of the discussion on the fragility of moral choices. A heightened moral awareness is the *ideal*, but the road to it is seen by ordinary people to lie in the consistent effort of self-improvement through attention to the proper (culturally defined) conduct of life. This is the process of maturation discussed in Chapter 1 in the context of the notion of the good life as Kashmiri Brahmans entertain it. While the pitfalls of making moral choices in a spirit of *ahaṁkāra* or hubris are recognized in Hindu culture (see Chapter 3), the importance of bringing what one desires (*preyas*) under the control of

[5] The Hindu notion of 'choiceless awareness', which perhaps appears exotic from a modern point of view, may, on reflection, not seem so strange after all. Consider the following observation by the philosopher Richard Wollheim, which parallels the idea of the gradual transition from deliberate choice-making to choiceless awareness through a process of maturation: 'My suggestion, then, is that the development of, or development beyond, the superego is best understood in this way: that the internal figure, or the group of internal figures, whose phantasized activities regulate the thoughts, feelings, and conduct of the person start off life as merely internalized figures—they "confront" the ego but, gradually, or at some rate depending upon circumstances, they come to be figures with whom the person is able to identify' (1984: 218).

what one ought to prefer (*śreyas*) is also stressed. In fact, the two perspectives are seen as mutually reinforcing rather than as contradictory. The moral effort involved is great, but failing to make the endeavour causes suffering. A traditional Hindu viewpoint is that he who thinks that he proclaims his freedom by defying cultural norms, in fact announces his servitude to impulses: ungoverned senses (*avaśyendriyaḥ*) indeed become the ruling passions, and ultimately lead to suffering (*duḥkha*). The theme of suffering, and of preparation for death, which are of central importance in Indian (Buddhist, Jaina, Hindu) world-views, are introduced in Chapter 4, but I have neither the data nor the scholarship to deal with the former at any length.

There is, however, one kind of human suffering—that associated with death—which I discuss in Chapter 5. A concern with longevity has long been present in Hindu culture, as in many other cultures: it goes back to Vedic times when the desire to live a hundred years was repeatedly voiced and associated with progeny and prosperity. It is not therefore surprising that the *brāhmaṇa* rituals were mostly concerned with prolonging life. There was also the idea of the possibility of exchanging an old body for a new one (see Chapter 3). The notion of the good life lived in the light of ethical norms became salient later on, but never completely displaced the value placed upon plenitude. Besides, the hope of postponing death through rituals gradually gave way to the philosophic attitude of the Upanishads. The notion of *karma* came to be recognized as the primary cause of birth and death. It also became the basis of the ethical doctrine of works and retribution: as the Brihadaranyaka Upanishad puts it, 'Verily, one becomes good through good deeds and evil through evil deeds' (III.ii.13).

Consequently, one is taught in the Hindu tradition to try to overcome evil, not to fear death. In fact, birth and death are not considered ontologically separate but recurrent events in a cosmo-moral process. Some anthropologists have defined birth as a latent root paradigm of Hindu culture. 'Each of the *saṁskāra*', Inden and Nicholas write, 'is an overt act of birth in a symbolic disguise' (1977: 91): I think they should have said 'an act of birth, death, rebirth . . .'. It is through such a philosophic notion, and the longing for and hope of divine grace (a still later idea than *karma*), that Hindus hope to cope with death and, indeed, elevate it to the status of being the final and most reliable witness to the good life.[6] But from the Hindu point of view the last moments of a life cannot outweigh or cancel all that has preceded them (though this happens in some mythological tales of divine grace). Performing rituals, seeking the intervention of saints, listening to holy scriptures, reliving old myths, and residing in sacred places (described in Chapter 5) are all supplementary devices, inferior to the philosophic attitude as a means to cope with death and the fear and suffering associated with it.

In the five chapters comprising the core of this book I have attempted to present interpretations of a tradition-based view of the life of the man-in-the-world as the good life in contrast to the life of the renouncer. I have made no mention of the fractured world of the 'modern' (and 'modernizing') Hindus, which is a curious medley of ancient monuments and half-formed new structures. Karl Marx diagnosed well the roots of the Hindu's melancholy: the 'loss of his old world with no gain of a new one' (Marx 1853). Their way of life, which the Hindus share at the margins with other non-Hindu Indians, is marked by uncertainties. The good life is now being defined in terms of borrowed criteria, namely, Western liberal ideals of material prosperity, political democracy, and secularism. The outlook on life of no modern Indian—neither of Tagore nor of Gandhi or Nehru—can be understood without taking India's encounter with the West into consideration—an encounter which has involved, first, the loss of the 'self' and, then, various attempts to recover it.[7] The quest for Hinduism, of which I write in the Epilogue, is part of this larger research for identity—and a major theme of so-called 'modern Indian

[6] Lamenting the absence of a notion of the 'good death' in contemporary American culture, Bateson writes: 'The timing of death, like the ending of a story, gives a changed meaning to what preceded it. Death is also the moment of a gift that the old give to the young, a last opportunity to teach about life, but is so shaped by accident and happenstance that the moment may pass and wisdom is often unexpressed' (1984: 206). Most Pandits would fully agree with the foregoing, though some might deny that 'accident and happenstance' have any place is human lives.

[7] One of the most insightful and interesting interpretations of this phenomenon of the loss and attempted recovery of the self among the 'modern' Hindus is that of the psychologist Ashis Nandy (1983).

culture'. I have thought it best to summon many witnesses, mostly Hindus, to present in their own words the predicament of the 'modern' Indian as they have individually or collectively viewed it. That my effort at interpretation of this phenomenon is inconclusive is, perhaps, a reflection of my own inadequacies as an interpreter, than of the present situation of the Hindu itself.

On the influences that make me the kind of author–interpreter I am, I would rather be silent. Were I to begin to identify them myself, I might soon run the risk of causing embarrassment to the very persons whom I would wish to thank. All I may say, therefore, is that I was born a Hindu and trained as a sociologist–social anthropologist. This combination has made me some kind of an 'insider–outsider' in relation to my own society (see Madan 1975b). There is nothing particularly unique about such a split (or compound) identity. And, as the psychoanalyst Sudhir Kakar says, 'boundary spaces between cultures are not necessarily bad places to live in' (1982: 9).

I

DOMESTICITY AND DETACHMENT

Why should we renounce the lovely world?
Our love of Him is our austerity . . .

KRISHNA RAZDAN

Deliverance is not for me in renunciation.
I feel the embrace of freedom in a thousand bonds of delight.

RABINDRANATH TAGORE

INTRODUCTORY

In a justly influential essay on renunciation in Indian religions, Louis Dumont suggested that 'the secret of Hinduism may be found in the dialogue between the renouncer and the man-in-the-world' (1960: 37f). Dumont was not, of course, the first person to draw attention to these two 'human types' in the Hindu universe: his contribution lay, rather, in his insistence that the renouncer and the man-in-the-world are best understood in terms of their relationship of opposition *and* complementarity. In this chapter (based on an essay written in honour of Louis Dumont) I make an effort to pursue his significant observation about 'the dialogue' by examining the place of the *gṛhastha* (householder) among the native Brahmans of Kashmir Valley, known generally as the Pandits.[1] I have described else-

[1] The word Pandit is, of course, the Sanskrit *paṇḍita* for scholar. The Pandits I know best are of the rural areas in the south-eastern part of the Kashmir Valley. Inquiries made over twenty odd years have convinced me that there is an impressive homogeneity in Pandit culture. Though the Pandits are divided into two sub-castes (priests and the others), and differences of socio-economic status and regional subculture also are found among them, these differences are not relevant in the context of the issues dealt with in this chapter, which are of the nature of the *principles* underlying social action rather than its *details* as observed in everyday life.

where at length (see Madan 1965) that the householder occupies the central place in everyday life in Pandit society: in fact, *he is the typical Pandit.* Here I try to delineate some crucial elements in the Pandit ideology of the householder.

It should be clarified here that, underlying the earlier account (Madan 1965), there was an implicit assumption of social relations as the basic phenomenon, which resulted in inadequate attention being paid to the cultural aspect of social reality. The corrective does not lie, of course, in replacing one parochialism, as it were, by another but, rather, in adopting a multidimensional approach to the interpretation of the data about everyday life. The study of ideas and beliefs must take place in the context of observable behaviour and *vice versa.*

Following Dumont (1957: 12), the kind of ideas I am interested in here are those that the Pandits themselves employ to bring out the purposiveness and meaningfulness of their institutions: ideas that embody norms and values, stating what is axiomatic and not to be questioned, but also enabling people to make choices in respect of both the purposes of human pursuits and the appropriate procedures for their fulfilment within the overall framework of *dharma.* Social relations may thus be seen as animated—whether sustained or altered—by such ideas.

There is need for caution, however, for, as Dumont (1980: 36f) has pointed out, ideas and values are not everything and they do not by themselves comprise socio-cultural reality, just as externally observable behaviour alone does not do so. While ideas provide the framework for the interpretation of behaviour, behaviour—that which actually happens—provides what Dumont (1977: 27) calls 'control', preventing the misunderstandings that an overweening emphasis on ideas alone might generate. In short, I am not setting up a mutually exclusive dichotomy of culture and society, but insisting that we recognize that social action is suffused with meaning and that intentions are central to it. Purposes are not causes, however, nor do I want to explain anything in confident teleological terms. This is an interpretive essay concerned with what Schutz (1976) calls 'constructs of typicalities'.

People's ideas are difficult to get at and analyse. They are not there for the ethnographer to pick up, as it were; he has to look for them and, indeed, ferret them out through intensive fieldwork. The ethnographic text is not a 'faithful' account of what has been seen and heard, but involves reconstruction and redescription—some scholars prefer to call it 'translation'—of what has been seen and heard, in the light of, first, people's own concepts of everyday life and its larger purposes and, second, the ethnographer's theoretical presuppositions about the nature of social life and the significance of people's ideas.

It is important that one seeks a fusion between the view from within (ideas, meanings) and the view from without (behaviour, rules), for anthropology is, as Dumont (1970: 157) has rightly pointed out, understanding born of the tension of these two perspectives. 'In this task', Dumont writes, 'it is not sufficient to translate the indigenous words, for it frequently happens that the ideas which they express are related to each other by more fundamental ideas *even though they are unexpressed.* Fundamental ideas literally "go without saying" and have no need to be distinct, that is tradition. Only their corollaries are explicit' (1957: 12).[2]

It is obvious that to achieve the foregoing objective, the ethnographer has to seek the companionship of informants in a joint endeavour of exploration of meaning in the minutiae of everyday life. Informants are not always forthcoming with general formulations. As Weber pointed out, 'actual action goes on in a state of inarticulate half-consciousness or actual unconsciousness of its subjective meaning' (1947: 111f). The reasonable assumption that one makes in this regard is that it is inconceivable that a person does not have a view of life and its purposes—*a weltanschauung*—even if he has not explicity formulated it. The point really is that he may be expected to formulate it. The ethnographer, therefore, invites the informants to reflect on their everyday life, discuss their behaviour, examine its purposes (not only the specific intentions that prompt particular actions but, and more importantly, general purposes also), evaluate procedures, and assign meanings. This may be done retrospectively as Schutz (1976) suggests.

In short, the ethnographer tries to formulate explicitly what

[2] Cf.: 'To be sure, the more standardized the prevailing action pattern is, the more anonymous it is, the greater is the subjective chance of conformity and, therewith, of the success of intersubjective behaviour' (Schutz 1967: 33).

the informants know implicitly and vaguely, perhaps only confusedly. His task is to connect and then redescribe what he observes and what he is told, without loss of meaning, and to interpret what is given in the informants' beliefs and their ready or coherent and not-so-coherent knowledge of their culture. Belief, knowledge and understanding are, of course, not one and the same thing.

Needless to emphasize, the ethnographer is not able to engage in and sustain such productive interaction with every informant. Fortunately, there are reflective individuals everywhere who are curious about their own culture and think about it.[3] But almost everyone—including children—contributes to the ethnographer's knowledge and understanding of the way of life he is attempting to understand. In the final synthesis that he endeavours to construct, the ethnographer assigns different kinds and degrees of significance to the various contributions, including his own, and establishes connection between them. This, then, is the manner in which the data embodied in this chapter were generated. It might be added that what I am dealing with here is, by and large, the Pandit oral tradition.[4]

[3] Schutz (1967: 61) refers to this phenomenon as the 'social distribution of knowledge': 'each individual knowing merely a sector of the world and common knowledge of the same sector varying individually as to its degree of distinctness, clarity, acquaintanceship, or mere belief'.

In this connexion I might add that my informants in the village of Utrassu-Umanagri, where most of my fieldwork has been done (see Madan 1965), accept without demur the fact that some of them know more than the others about certain matters. One does not question what one does not know but seeks clarifications about it from others. I have, for instance, written elsewhere about the general lack of interest in genealogical materials among the Pandits combined with a deep interest in them on the part of some (see Madan 1975b: 141–6).

[4] I would like to explain that, though nearly all the adult male Pandits of Utrassu-Umanagri during the late 1950s were literate, not more than a dozen could claim proficiency in Sanskrit or scholarship in traditional literature dealing with metaphysical problems or ritual performances. The priests, of course, had a reading knowledge of Sanskrit, particularly in the *śāradā* script, but the few true *paṇḍita* who lived in the village were from among the non-priestly families. Not many households possessed any books other than almanacs and children's schoolbooks. The most commonly found 'religious' texts were the Bhagavad Gita and books of prayers and hymns. A few households owned astrological books. The epics—the Mahabharata and the Ramacharitamanas—were also found in some homes, not always in the original Sanskrit or Avadhi but in Urdu prose

SOCIOCULTURAL IDENTITY: '*Bhaṭṭil*' AND '*Gārhasthya*'

Selfhood and personhood

To give a systematic account of the Pandit ideology of the householder, it seems appropriate to begin with the Pandit conception of socio-cultural identity—of 'personhood'—for even those who may not be householders are yet Pandits, members of the community (*barādarī*, the 'fraternity').[5] Some Pandits among the many I have talked with about the presuppositions of their culture have emphasized the importance of going deeper than the level of personhood (man-in-society) and attending to what they consider the most fundamental notion of all, namely 'selfhood', expressed in the ancient question, 'Who am I?' According to the Pandits, what distinguishes human beings from other sentient beings is their capacity for introspection (*cintan*) and self-realization (*ātmajñāna*). Though most Pandits are only dimly aware of the monistic teaching of Kashmir Shaivism (see Chatterji 1914), many affirm identity with Shiva —*Śivoham*, I am Shiva!—as the true goal of the seeker and, therefore, the only valid answer to the question of selfhood. This is, however, by no means a general concern and occupies only the cognoscenti.

When confronted by me with the foregoing formulation, the majority of the Pandits I have talked with averred that such knowledge (*jñāna*) is beyond the comprehension of the common man and of not much avail to him, enmeshed as he is in 'the veil of illusion' (*māyā-jāl*) of everyday life. This is stated more in a matter-of-fact way than in a self-deprecatory tone. They assert that the inward-looking emphasis on selfhood is not the common man's problem: his concern is the proper performance

---

translations. Centuries of persecution at the hands of Muslim rulers had already brought the Pandits of Kashmir to this sad pass by the middle of the nineteenth century when Hindu rule was re-established. This is why I have chosen to describe the Pandit tradition as 'oral'. A lament on the decline of the Pandit literary tradition remains to be written.

[5] '*Barādarī*' is a Persian word. Most Kashmiri words are of either Sanskrit or Persian derivation, but the difference in pronunciation between the original and the derivative words is often considerable. Thus, Kashmiris hardly ever use aspirated consonant sounds. For the sake of comparability of the linguistic material, I have used the original Sanskrit or Persian words whenever I could identify these (see Kachru 1973).

of social roles (*duniyā-dārī*, 'world-maintenance') in consonance with *dharma*. In other words, it is the pressing, if not the paramount, reality of everyday life, demanding constant attention and action, which is the primary concern of most Pandits and, they believe, of most human beings. (Whether this is fortunate or unfortunate, the Pandits maintain, is another question.) And the householder is the *duniyā-dār* (man-in-the-world) *par excellence*. In the context of such an involvement in everyday life, answering the question 'Who am I?' still remains important, but from the perspective of social interaction or personhood rather than withdrawal from society and selfhood.

Apropos personhood, two initial questions may now be posed. First, how does one know a person to be a Pandit? Second, how do the Pandits themselves define their socio-cultural identity and communicate it to others when the need for doing so arises?

External signs of Pandit identity

The Pandits refer to themselves, and are referred to by other Kashmiri-speaking people, as the Bhaṭṭa. The word is of Sanskrit origin and means a learned person and one who is concerned with communicating or the telling of what there is to know.[6] Needless to say, not every Pandit is a scholar, or in possession of esoteric knowledge, and the etymology of the word *bhaṭṭa* is of no practical significance. It is simply used to designate those Kashmiris who are not Muslims or Sikhs.

There are many outward signs of recognition of a Pandit and of places and events associated with him. The traditional clothing of Pandit men, women and children is different from that of their Muslim co-villagers. Though a non-Kashmiri might not easily recognize these differences in the case of men and children—there can be no mistaking a married Pandit woman's traditional or contemporary sartorial style for that of anyone else's—the Kashmiris themselves perceive them readily. Also, many Pandits, particularly women, wear the very visible *tyok* on their forehead—a mark made with sandalwood or rosewood paste, saffron, or *sindūr* (vermilion), or mixtures of these.

[6] *Bhaṭṭa* is the Prakrit form of the Sanskrit *bhartṛ*, the honorific designation of learned Brahmans—it is a synonym of *paṇḍita*. It may be noted here that Kashmiri has been classified as a *prākrita*.

When bare-headed, a Pandit man or boy may be recognized by his tuft of head-top hair (*chog*), but this is now less commonly found than it was a couple of generations ago. An adult Pandit male, who has stripped himself to the waist for a wash, or some other purpose, will always be recognized by the holy cord of three cotton strands (*yonya* or *yajñopavīta*)—characteristic of the twice-born castes all over India—worn round the neck, or round the neck and under the right arm.

Pandit houses look different from those of other Kashmiris, both inside and from outside. Their places of worship also are distinctive in appearance, as are their religious, wedding and funeral gatherings. The sight of flowers (particularly marigolds) and the sound of conch shells are characteristic of these events. Though they speak Kashmiri like the others, the Pandits' speech is more laden with Sanskrit than that of Muslims. Personal and family names, with a few exceptions, are also different.[7]

Most Pandit households earn their livelihood from land, service of various types (including domestic and government service), and/or trade. Such Pandits are called *Kārkun* ('those who work for profit'). A small minority carve out their living as priests (*Gor*) and are also referred to as the *Bhāṣā* (language, i.e., Sanskrit) *Bhaṭṭa*. The *Kārkun* and the *Gor* do not intermarry. The Pandits do not perform any of the functions associated with artisan or service castes in other parts of India: it is the Kashmiri Muslims who perform all these tasks. The Pandits and Muslims are linked by co-residence in villages (or in urban neighbourhoods) and by economic transactions. There are no marriage and commensal relations between them and physical contact is severely restricted. Agreement between the communities is built upon an explicit recognition of differences between them (see Madan 1972). For the Pandits, the Muslims are the 'others' or 'outsiders' (*mleccha*) but not strangers (*vopar*), and *vice versa*.

[7] While no Pandit would have a personal name of Islamic origin, a secular word like the Persian *āftāb* (sun) or *mahtāb* (moon) was used in the past: there was a Mahtab Kaula in Utrassu-Umanagri in 1957–8. This points to Muslim (Persian and Afghan) cultural elements in Pandit culture, of which there is evidence in domestic architecture, music, food, clothing, speech, etc. Similarly, Kashmiri Muslims preserve many relics of their Hindu ancestry in their culture, the most interesting, or perhaps ironical, being the fact that a common family name among them is Bhat; there are some Muslim 'Pandit' families also.

Pandit identity: self-ascription

By themselves the Pandits constitute not merely a single breed (*bīja* or *byol*, 'seed') but, more significantly, one *zāt*. The notion of *zāt* is subtler than that of the community of kith and kin and common customary behaviour. In fact, the word is used in two senses. Generally and rather loosely, it connotes the family name or the name of an occupational group. It is also used to convey the particular idea that a people (*quom*, the anthropologists' ethnic group), whether Pandits or any other, ultimately are what they are and do what they do because of their essential and inborn, but alterable, nature. Soils, plants, animals, human beings, gods—all have their *zāt* or essence. Among human beings it is considered to be a product of physical and moral elements: in fact, it may well be understood as the hierarchical relation between the two, with the moral element encompassing the physical. One's *zāt* may become refined through appropriate effort—what Marriott (1977) calls the process of maturation—or it may become corrupted through the neglect of moral duties. As an informant once put it to me, 'a Pandit is not the fruit of the pursuit of pleasure (*kāma*) but of moral duty (*dharma*)'. The reference is to the paramount duty of the householder to beget children—particularly sons—so that the lineage (*kula*) is continued and the manes are assured offerings of water (*treś*, *tarpaṇa* 'quenching of thirst', 'satiating') and food (*piṇḍa*) and their perdition is averted. In the process, the Pandit community also survives.

A Pandit is thus born a Pandit and there is no other way of acquiring this identity. One loses it by totally abandoning the traditional way of life, or the crucial elements of it, as when one eats and lives with Muslims or marries among them. Such actions result in a crucial alteration (deterioration) of one's *zāt*. A Pandit must, therefore, guard it always. I once asked a Pandit who had become a Muslim why he had done so. His answer was that it was a flaw in his *karma* that blinded him and made him go astray. I do not mean to suggest that every Pandit converted to Islam has such regrets: such conversions are, in any case, extremely rare. The point, rather, is that one who is repentant should think about it in terms of a moral lapse, a falling away from *dharma*, and, I might add, the consequent deterioration of one's *zāt*. Despite his regret, this man never mentioned the hope of a restoration of his lost status. He knew this loss to be irrevocable. And the Pandits of his village saw in him a fallen man—a very pitiable creature.

The significant relation between moral and physical elements in the make-up of a person does not mean the denial of importance to the physical foundation of personhood. On the contrary, it is dramatized at the beginning of all major rituals when the person performing a rite summons himself into existence, as it were, by pointing to and naming different parts of his body, beginning with his feet and culminating in his head, and purifying them by sprinkling water on them with blades of the purifying *darbha* grass (*Poa cynosuroides*).

Parenthood: biology and morality

According to the Pandits, the fact that sexual intercourse does not always lead to conception may be because of some bodily deficiency of the wife or husband. Barrenness is recognized as a physical incapacity, which may, however, have karmic causes. A childless wife may be jokingly advised by her friends to change her 'cover' or quilt (*vurun*)—that is, sleep with a man other than her husband—but this would, of course, be a reprehensible breach of moral conduct. Barrenness among women and infertility among men may be produced by disease, sorcery or the curse of people endowed with supernatural powers. But, ultimately, whether a couple will or will not be blessed with children, the much sought after sons in particular, is a question of fate (*prārabdha*), of *karma-lekhā* (the 'written', or the pre-ordained, results of one's actions in the previous life). In the normal course of events, there is no escape from the consequences of one's actions; only divine grace (*anugraha*) can come to one's rescue, but this is hard to obtain.

It is generally maintained that conception occurs when husband and wife reach orgasm simultaneously. Female orgasm is believed to result in the discharge of vital fluids into the womb which also receives the male 'seed'. Not only were my informants uncertain about the nature of the supposed female discharge, some of them also considered it to be of no consequence. The male seed is believed to contain in it all the requirements for the making of the complete human being: flesh, blood, all internal and external organs, hair, nails, intellect, knowledge, ignorance, health, disease, etc. It has the capacity to provide for the nurture of the foetus and subsequently of the new-born child. The mother's menstrual blood provides the 'soil' or 'bed' for the seed to grow in when it ceases to flow out and solidifies into the fleshy 'sack' which envelops and nourishes the foetus. It is because of this fact, some informants said, that Hindus have adopted the black stone *śālagrāma*, which resembles the womb in shape, as the iconic representation of Vishnu, the preserver. The growth of the child's body, which is already in the seed, depends upon the mother and her physical and moral condition. The original planting of the seed in the womb sets in process the milk-producing capacity of the mother who then suckles the child when it is born. In short, as one informant put it, the human seed is very much like the walnut which contains in itself the full-grown tree—incidentally the largest fruit-bearing tree in Kashmir.

Despite the potency of the male seed, the father's role is seen as rather accidental and episodic compared to the mother's sustained and intimate involvement with the child during both the pre-natal and post-natal stages. A Kashmiri proverb bluntly proclaims this intimacy: 'illegitimate or legitimate, I carried the child for nine months in my own womb'. In other words, while the physical bond between father and child may never be proven, there can be little doubt about it in the case of mother and child. Human life, the Pandits aver, consists of the obligation to repay debts (*ṛṇa*) incurred in the course of numerous lives: debts to gods, ancestors (including one's father), teachers, fellow human beings.

There is one debt, however, which never gets repaid because it cannot be repaid: this is the debt one owes one's mother (*mātṛ-ṛṇa*). There is no one—not excepting one's father, not even God—obedience to whom is enjoined more strictly on human beings than to one's mother. All one's kith and kin, including the father, may turn wicked, but the bad mother (*kumātā*) is unknown.[8] The bond between mother and child

[8] Stepmothers are, however, different. They are generally said to be cruel to the children of their husband's deceased wife, particularly when they have children

is the moral bond of love *par excellence*—Fortes's axiom of amity (Fortes 1969: 219ff)—unsullied by the kinds of mundane considerations that enter into the father–son relationship. The Kashmiri woman is said to be a child-worshipper (*baca-parast*). The reverence for human mothers is paralleled by the Pandits' veneration for mother goddesses, particularly their patron goddesses Sharika and Ragnya, both addressed as *jagadambā*, 'universal mother', whom they accord a higher place in the divine hierarchy than their divine consorts. Mothers thus pervade both the human and the divine spheres.

Fathers also are obviously important: 'the seed flows clearing the way for the flow of property' is how an informant summed up the biological and social significance of the father–son bond. When I suggested to him (and other informants) that the way that the flow of 'seed' clears is not only for the downward transmission of property but also for the upward flow of food offerings (*piṇḍa*), they agreed with me. But there is a problem in respect of the father–child relationship. The mother has milk and she gives it all to her children. A woman may even die in childbirth, sacrificing her life for the sake of the child. The father has property and he shares it with his sons; in fact, he may try to deny this obligation. The mother gives absolutely of what she has, but the father does so only partially or conditionally: it is here that the seeds of household conflict often lie (see Madan 1965: chap. 8).

The father–child relationship is moral, even as the mother–child bond is, but it also has a material dimension: not only do sons share ancestral property with their father and inherit his share in it, daughters also receive a dowry and post-nuptial prestations from their natal family (see Madan 1975a: 231–41). Inheritance by sons and gifts to daughters (and their conjugal families) are governed by law and custom, and these may often be manipulated by particular individuals to suit their own

---

of their own. I even heard stories about the attempts of some women to poison their stepchildren. Adoptive mothers are unpredictable. If a child has been foisted upon the issueless woman by her husband's relatives, she may not feel very attached to it, but mothers do often treat their adopted children with the same love and care as natural mothers do. Between the 'pangs of bearing' (*zenadod*) and 'the toils of rearing' (*racchandod*), the Pandits aver, it is hard to arbitrate, but in the ultimate analysis 'blood simmers in one's veins'.

advantage. The Pandits often justify the actions of a son who fights his father over property, blaming the older man for such vices as covetousness or intolerance of others' points of view. They never condone the neglect by a son of the material needs of his mother, even if she is a stepmother. Leach's contention (see Leach 1961: 9) that economic constraints are prior to the constraints of kinship morality does not hold good of the mother–child relationship among the Pandits; it applies to the father–son relationship but only at the level of behaviour and not in terms of kinship ideology, in which filial piety is extolled as an imperative of *dharma*.

Property endures, as Leach (1961: 11) has pointed out, but so do the moral bonds between parents and children. An adult Pandit's first action in the morning, after he has performed ablutions and before he eats any solid food—the pious will not even drink anything—is to offer water to quench the 'thirst' (*treś*) of his manes, beginning with his own deceased parents. Moreover, twice a year he performs the *śrāddha* ritual for his parents on their respective death anniversaries (according to the Hindu lunar calender) and on the appropriate days during the annual fortnight-long 'feeding' of manes (*kāmbar-paccha*). *Piṇḍa* (conically shaped lumps of cooked rice) are offered to them symbolically and thrown into flowing waters or fed to birds after the ritual. Invited priests are then fed the favourite dishes of the deceased parents.

Other ancestors also receive *piṇḍa*: five lineal male ascendants beginning with one's father's father, on the occasion of the father's *śrāddha*, and father's mother, father's father's mother and so on up to the father's fourth lineal male ascendant's mother (FaFaFaFaFaMo), on the occasion of the mother's *śrāddha*. Still other ancestors, notably the mother's father, may also be offered *piṇḍa*, or—this is more likely—dry, uncooked rice, salt and fruits (called *sīddha*) may be given to the family priest in the name of the dead person. Those to whom one normally offers *piṇḍa* or *sīddha*, and their descendants, are one's *sapiṇḍa*: one is related to them through the ritual food offering, and a man must not take a wife from among them, or give a daughter or sister in marriage to them, within the limits defined by the food offering.[9] It is obvious that the Pandits dis-

[9] Legal texts translate the word *sapiṇḍa* to mean those 'connected by particles of

approve of the mixing together or confusion of categories, the basic distinction in this context being between wife-givers and wife-takers (see Madan 1965: 105; 1975a), with others derived from it.

The nature of the parent–child relationship is thus specified in *dharma*, which declares the moral basis of the relationship and defines what its content should be. The Pandits are down-to-earth pragmatists and acknowledge that the dictates of *dharma* are often violated by people. Why should this be so? Why should considerations of economic gain emerge blatantly as prior to the dictates of morality in some cases? The Pandit answer is, '*havālayat*', that is, the notion that you may receive from your children what you gave unto them (to keep in 'safe custody', as it were) in the previous life. In short, it is *karma*.

Fate (*prārabdha*) informs the parent–child relationship at every step: from the initial step of *kanyādāna* (the gift of a maiden by her father to her chosen husband), through the intermediate step of *garbhādāna* (the receiving of the seed by the wife from the husband), to the ultimate step of *piṇḍadāna* (the post-mortuary gift of food by a son to his parents and other ancestors). This threefold pattern of gifts, given and received, is the defining characteristic of the domain of kinship and domesticity among the Pandits, forming the basis of a person's relations with (to borrow Schutz's terminology once again) his predecessors, consociates and successors. More generally, it is the very basis of the Pandit way of life and of the definition of cultural identity. Birth and death are physiological events found among all sentient beings. It is the specific cultural expression of these events, and what precedes, accompanies and follows them, that defines a Pandit and distinguishes him not only from all living beings but also and specifically from non-Pandits. Ethnophysiology, morality, ritual, custom

one body' (see, e.g., Mayne 1950: 146); in doing so they follow Vijñāneśvara's twelfth-century text, known as the Mitākṣara. It would seem that this usage is also commonly employed by Hindus in Bengal in defining the category of 'one's own people', who are seen related to oneself as *eka-śārira* or *sapiṇḍa*, that is, by the 'same body' (Inden and Nicholas 1977: 3). The literal meanings of the word *piṇḍa*, it must be noted, include not only 'body' but also 'balls of cooked rice' offered to manes.

and law—all these are elements in the definition of identity and of the cultural idiom in which it is expressed.

'Bhaṭṭil' : traditional purposes of life

The Pandits' conception of socio-cultural identity is given explicit expression in their notion of '*bhaṭṭil*', the *Bhaṭṭa* way of life. Needless to emphasize, they consider *bhaṭṭil* the best, that is, morally the most superior, way of life. It is constituted of a range of fundamental purposes of life (*puruṣārtha* or *abhiprāya*) largely centred in domestic life, and of appropriate procedures for their fulfilment. These purposes and procedures have their basis in tradition. When children—the great questioners in every society—and even curious adults ask of those who might know why something should be done in a particular manner, or done at all, the Pandit answer usually is: 'it is *bhaṭṭil*; it is our way of life'. If the questioner persists and demands a fuller answer, he is sought to be silenced by the utterance of the single exclamatory word '*ada!*'. As an affirmatory exclamation, '*ada*' would mean, 'that is the way it is', implying that 'this is the way it should be'. Put negatively, the connotation would be: 'there is no reason', implying that 'no reason need be given'. '*Ada*' could also be interpreted as a counter-question: 'What else is the way?' or 'why should I tell you?'

The foregoing gloss, I must clarify, is my attempt to decode this powerful verbal symbol on the basis of careful attention to the contexts and manner of its use. My informants never explained the term to me but left me in no doubt about its significance. It stands for the virtue (not merely an attitude) of unquestioning acceptance of the moral imperative. It is not employed in connection with the inevitability of natural or physiological processes, such as the change of seasons or death. There were many among my informants—the inevitable sceptics—who considered the notion of '*ada*' an expression of ignorance and/or irrationality; as they sarcastically put it, 'there is no higher *śāstra* among the *Bhaṭṭa* than the *ada-śāstra*'. It is obvious that we are here confronted with axiomatic truths which are the foundation of tradition everywhere. These truths were never stated to me in any systematic form by my informants. Certain overarching notions have, nevertheless, emerged quite clearly in the course of my conversations with individual Pandits and through group discussions. I now turn to some of these notions relevant to my present concern.

A Pandit's most precious possession, I have been repeatedly told, is his self. One's self is, of course, more than one's body (*śarīra*). The physical self or the body by itself is really of little significance. It is fragile, subject to deterioration, and readily perishable: it is *kṣaṇabhaṅgur*—that which may disintegrate any moment. It is when the body is joined to the inner self (*antarātma*) that it becomes the vehicle of *dharma*. It is, therefore, not the body but the network of dharmic relations that really matters. Thus the backbone of the family and the lineage is the relationship between ascendants and descendants in the male line affirmed in the *śrāddha*. He who neglects this first principle of treating the body as a means in the achievement of purposes beyond the body, and not an end in itself, turns out to be, in the words of an informant (who switched from Kashmiri to Hindi), '*tīn janama kā bhūkhā*', that is, one who remains spiritually starved through three lives—the previous, the present and the future. One's present life's difficulties indicate the neglect of *dharma* in the previous one; one's present failures ensure the difficulties of the next one. How does one meet this primary obligation of spiritual advancement? Through steadfast adherence to *bhaṭṭil* in whatever one does and in the manner one does it.

The demands of nature, while the body lasts, are not to be denied but fulfilled in accordance with *bhaṭṭil*. When this is done, one acquires fame (*yaś*) for righteous conduct in this world (*ihaloka*) and merit for the next (*paraloka*). The body is thus the meeting ground of the past, the present and the future; to put it differently, the present is the link between the past and the future. What one does with one's body and how the present is filled are then, obviously, matters of great import.

In the context of this concern, it is important to note that the Pandits' whole way of life is pervaded by a sense of auspiciousness (*śubha*) and purity (*śuddha*, *śauca*) and, consequently, by the fear of inauspiciousness and a concern with impurity.[10] While inauspiciousness (signified by such happenings as deaths, eclipses, the hooting of owls, etc.) is generally considered to be

[10] See chapter 2 below.

beyond human control, the threat of contamination by impurity is seen to lie primarily in the manner in which a Pandit may be tempted to attend to the needs arising from his physical nature, from the fact of his being a sentient being (*jīva*). Hence the obsessive emphasis on the questioning attitude, the exercise of doubt (*śaṅkā*). The Pandit is a doubter because he is a believer. I have heard many Pandits say in good-humoured self-deprecation that their hesitations in relation to the pursuit of worldly pleasures are the result of doubt or uncertainty about the consequences of indulging the senses for one's higher pursuits. The Pandit is enjoined to exercise patience and restraint (*ced*), and to be ever prepared to resist the compulsions of bodily appetites until assured of their proper satisfaction as defined in *bhaṭṭil*. Thus, it is '*ced*' that marks one out as a Pandit: this is his obligation as also his privilege. Man is endowed with *citta* (moral consciousness) and must cultivate it to resolve his doubts, or else he will lose it and become *jaḍa* (one lacking in the capacity for discrimination) or even an *unamatta* (one distorted in intellect).

Their chequered history[11] has, however, taught the Pandits that there are exceptional circumstances when the need for compromise arises and one is constrained to violate the requirements of *bhaṭṭil*. As stated above, and elsewhere in detail (see Madan 1972), there are no Hindu artisan and service castes in rural Kashmir and the Pandits are obliged to accept the help of Muslims—not only of butchers, cobblers and cultivators but also of washermen, barbers, milkmen and others. Contact with Muslims is a threat to the Pandits' state of personal and domestic purity. Though the Pandits avoid intimate physical contact of all kinds with Muslims, indirect contact is either unavoidable (for example, the services of a barber or of the attendant at the cremation ground) or is tolerated (for example, acceptance of milk from a Muslim cowherd or having one's house cleaned by a Muslim servant). There is no solution to this problem and the Pandits say: '*yath na puś, tath na duś*', 'whereof one is helpless, thereof one is blameless'.

[11] Since the coming of Islam in the fourteenth century, Kashmiri Hindus have had to live off their wits and on compromises. It is remarkable that they should have survived at all. For an account of the vicissitudes through which they have passed see Bamzai (1962).

The same is true of all unwitting breaches of proper conduct. Minor lapses, such as unavoidable physical contact with Muslims in certain situations, can be taken care of by the performance of routine corrective actions, such as washing of one's hands (*śuddhi*). In more serious cases (such as the inadvertent eating of strictly forbidden foods), one must perform *prāyaścitta* (a ritual of atonement), though I have never witnessed one. Purificatory rites are, however, quite common.

The questioning attitude (*śaṅkā*), the exercise of restraint (*ced*), and the cultivation of the moral consciousness (*citta*), then, provide the framework within which a Pandit has to order his life: thoughtful discrimination (*vicāra*) must be the basis of conduct (*ācāra*). The pursuit of *dharma* is not a call to an exercise in abstraction: it is in the everyday life of economic pursuits (*artha*) and bodily appetites (*kāma*) that *dharma* has to prevail. This is what *bhaṭṭil* is all about. In Dumont's terms, *dharma* must encompass *artha* and *kāma*.[12] This hierarchical balance of *puruṣārtha* can be achieved only in the life of the householder, which is, therefore, the most highly valued identity of a human being in the Pandit scheme of life and values.

The Pandits' attitude to worldly concerns and rewards is one of joyful acceptance. They do not seek immediate release (*mokṣa*) from them, in the present life, but try to accumulate merit for the future. *Karma* is the chain of bondage, but it is not for this reason alone unwelcome. What is important, many informants said, is the attitude of surrender to God (*śaraṇabhāva*) and the elimination of ego (*ahaṁkāra*). Here and now the Pandits strive for health, wealth and progeny, and pray for divine blessing in the fulfilment of these wishes. When a man kneels with folded hands before a priest to have his forehead marked with vermilion or saffron, the latter pronounces a blessing (in Sanskrit):

May you be long lived, may you be blessed with sons, may you be wealthy, may you be renowned, may you be wise, may you be greatly

[12] 'There are three "human ends", *dharma*, *artha* and *kāma*, duty, profit, and pleasure. All three are (necessary and) lawful, but they are so graded in a hierarchy that an inferior ideal may be pursued only as far as a superior one does not intervene: *dharma*, conformity to the world order, is more important than *artha*, power and wealth, which in turn is above *kāma*, immediate enjoyment' (Dumont 1960: 41).

prosperous, may you be possessed with full faith in mercy and charity, may you be glorious, may you be one who lowers the pride of his enemies, may you be ingenious in trade, may you always be devoted to worshipping the feet of God, may you do good to all!

Similarly, a married woman receives her blessing: 'May you be blessed with money and sons, may you be devoted and faithful to your husband, may you always be dearly loved by your husband, may you be insightful, may you have correct understanding, may you live a hundred years!' Those who have their wishes fulfilled in good measure see in that the sign of previous good *karma* and also of divine grace: the two always go together.

The purposes of life are, then, well established in tradition. The emphasis is upon dharmic striving for worldly goals. 'Woman (*strī*) and wealth (*dhana*)', said an informant, 'are the means by which the householder is able to perform virtuous actions (*dharma-kāj*); but a man's undoing also are woman (as *kāminī*, that is, as the object of lust) and greed for gold (*kāncan*). It is, indeed, like walking on the razor's edge of which the seers (*ṛṣi*) have spoken.' Plenitude is to be rejoiced in, but only within the bounds defined in *bhaṭṭil*. To quote the same informant again, 'where indulgence is, *bhaṭṭil* is not'.

'*Bhaṭṭil*': *traditional procedures*

The most comprehensive concept of social action is that of ordered conduct. It consists of such general notions as customs and conventions (*rīti*), procedures (*vidhi*) and daily routine (*niyam* or *nityakarma*). Then there are the specialized technical acts (*kriyā*) that help one to awaken one's dormant power (*śakti*), but these are only for the adepts. A very important component of such ordered conduct is the cycle of rituals (*saṁskāra*)—the so-called *rites de passage*—which must be performed in respect of each individual, in a prescribed sequence, beginning before birth and ending only after death. The proper locus for all these actions is the home, where 'the three fires of domestic life' burn: these are the fire in the hearth, the fire lit periodically to perform rituals, and 'the fire that is (or should be) always alight in one's own body (*deha*)—the fire of righteous actions'.

To mention the main life-cycle rituals, there are the childhood rituals of purification (*kaha nethar*, performed on the eleventh day after birth), the feeding of the first solid meal (*annaprāśana*), the first tonsure (*zarakāsai*, for boys only), the piercing of earlobes (*kancombani*, nowadays for girls only), and the investiture of boys with the holy girdle (*mekhalā*) and the holy neck cord (*yajñopavīta*).[13] Marriage (*nethar*, that which cannot be changed or undone) is the principal *saṁskāra* of adult life. The ultimate rite is that of cremation (*dāhasaṁskāra*), which is followed by post-mortuary rites. The general purpose of these rituals is to invest the person with the ritual status of a Brahman, to enlarge the repertoire of the roles that men or women may perform while alive, and to ensure their well-being as manes after their death. This is the so-called process of maturation. Marriage stands out as the central ritual and social event in the life of every individual, enabling him or her to take on the highly valued role of a householder. In the performance of all these rituals, the householder is helped by his family priest, who is an adept in the procedures. In fact, his presence at these rituals is absolutely essential.

Saṁskāras are dramatic events which involve all or most adult members and also some children of a household in different roles. By contrast, the routine chores and rites of everyday life—the so-called *nityakarma*—are the abiding concerns of the individual Pandit and constitute an important and ever-present element of his *bhaṭṭil*. Limitations of space preclude a detailed account of these and I will mention only the main types of these activities. It is with the proper performance of ablutions (*śaucācāra*) and the offering of water for the satisfaction of the manes (*tarpaṇa*) that every day should begin. Prayers and offerings to gods and goddesses—especially to one's 'favourites', the *iṣṭadeva* or *iṣṭadevī*—may take place at home or at a sacred place outside, such as beside flowing water or in a

[13] What is called the *upanayana* ceremony elsewhere in north India is called *mekhalā*, or *yajñopavīta*, among the Pandits, and very great importance is attached to it both as a ritual and as a social event. It takes place usually in the seventh or ninth year of a boy's life. In all twenty-four rites are performed on the occasion, beginning with *bijavāpānam*, for ensuring the fertility of the parents of the boy, which may not have been performed, as it should have been, in the father's twenty-fifth and the mother's sixteenth year. All other rites, which should have been but may or may not have been performed, are also performed, culminating in the investiture of the girdle (*mekhalā*) and the holy neck cord (*yajñopavīta*).

temple. There is much individual and day-to-day variation in this regard. One may only read or recite from memory some sacred texts (such as the Shivamahimnastotram, in praise of Shiva, the Bhavanisahasranama, in priase of Devi, or the Bhagavad Gita)—this is called *pāṭh*; or one may also perform a ritual of adoration (*pūjā*) of the traditional iconic representations of Vishnu, Shiva and Devi, namely the *śālagrāma*, *liṅga* and *śrīyantra* respectively. *Nityakarma* also includes the observance of birth and death anniversaries (the *śrāddha* is of very great importance to the Pandits), the eating of proper foods cooked properly (though the Pandits do not observe vegetarianism, the dietary restrictions they observe are numerous), the discharge of social obligations (such as visiting kith and kin to offer felicitations or condolences), etc.

As in the case of *saṁskāra*, the concern in *nityakarma* is with the protection of one's personal moral and physical well-being and the establishment and maintenance of the right kinds of relationships between kith and kin, the living and the dead, and human beings and deities. The cycle of daily activities is assessed in the context of transmigration: does it add to the burden of the *karma* of previous lives or lighten it? The heavier the load of sins (*pāpa*), which alone could make the curses (*śāpa*) pronounced by others effective, the greater the chances of suffering as retribution. The Pandit view of life is moralistic: whatever the immediate agency that brings about good fortune or misfortune, ultimately it is the inexorable law of *karma* that is believed to govern human life. A person must not blame his woes on God, for, as an informant put it, 'God does not discriminate between human beings and hand out joy to some and sorrow to others.'

It is, therefore, imperative to follow the straight path of *dharma* in its various expressions. One can do nothing better about the future than mind the present, for it is the dialectic of the past and the present *karma* that determines one's future. The content of one's accumulated *karma* is, therefore, of utmost importance: there is scope for choices made in the light of a cultivated moral consciousness so that a person's actions may be such as to render him deserving of divine grace. It is in this sense that a person may aspire to be a 'doer' (*karmavān*), a moral agent. Otherwise, he remains tied to the wheel of *karma* interminably, 'born again, to die again, to be conceived once again'. A person attains release from his sins only very gradually through the performance of duties in full consciousness and in the attitude of submission to the divinity.[14] Meanwhile, one seeks selfless joy in the proper pursuit of the legitimate purposes of life. In the words of the nineteenth-century poet-saint, Parmananda, which have often been quoted and sung to me, 'let the performance of *karma* be firmly grounded in *dharma*: sow the seed of contentment (*santoṣa*) and reap the harvest of joy (*ānanda*)'.

ALTERNATIVE ORIENTATIONS

I have tried to show above that implicit in the Pandit ideology of *bhaṭṭil* is the belief that, while all sentient beings are subject to natural law ('they are born and they die'), human beings are additionally constrained by moral imperatives which are not, however, equally developed among all people. According to the Pandits, among the best of these moralities—if not the only one—is *bhaṭṭil*. As we have seen, *bhaṭṭil* finds its most elaborate expression in the life of the householder. This does not, however, mean that the Pandits do not recognize any alternatives to the householder's way of life: they acknowledge the virtue of *virakti* (detachment) or *sannyāsa* (renunciation), but notionally rather than in practice. It is, however, neither considered necessary nor a better path to become worthy of receiving divine blessing, nor is it, in fact, a commonly chosen way of life. More about this below. What must be emphasized here is that the Pandits maintain that good *karma* and divine grace, rather than austerity, are what matter ultimately.

Bhakti

The Pandit is content to live the live of a householder and seek virtue and salvation through doing so properly. The

[14] Cf. 'The knowledge of the Absolute, *parā vidyā*, which secures immediate liberation (*sadyo-mukti*) is possible only for those who are able to withdraw their thoughts from worldly objects and concentrate on the ultimate fact of the universe. The knowledge of Īśvara (the Supreme as God), *aparā vidyā*, puts one on the pathway that leads to deliverance eventually (*krama-mukti*). The worshipping soul gradually acquires the higher wisdom which results in the consciousness of the identity with the Supreme' (Radhakrishnan 1953: 579).

householder's life is, as we have seen, defined (that is, bounded) by moral imperatives and procedures of various kinds. The danger of lapses and the fear of their consequences is, therefore, always present. Hence the Pandit notions of *gārhasthya* as an ordeal (*tapa*) and the supreme sacrifice (*mahāyajña*). The only way to lighten this burdensomeness of *bhaṭṭil*, the Pandits say, is through *bhakti*. *Bhakti* is a complex notion involving love of, and deep devotion to, the divinity and the seeking of refuge through the abolition of egotism.

Bhakti is not an alternative way of life but a particular orientation of the householder's life, 'away from the love of the world towards the love of God'. The Pandits consider *bhakti* as a value in itself. 'Filling one's self with the love of divinity', 'like a vessel may be filled with nectar', is an act which is its own reward. Of course, if the divinity grants it, the devotee (*bhakta*) will be bestowed with the capacity for right thought and conduct and thus liberated. The expression used for liberation in this context is '*moklāvun*', which literally means 'terminating' or 'freeing', the reference being to the ending of the cycle of birth, death and rebirth. Such is the nature of divine blessing (*anugraha*). The Pandits say that the special characteristic of *kaliyuga* among the four aeons of cosmic time is that a devotee does not have to engage in severe and long drawn-out austerities (*tapasyā*) to win divine favour. They maintain that 'if the devotee's heart breaks from the pangs of separation from the divinity for just as long as a hailstone will stay on the tip of a bull's horn', divine grace will be assured. But such is the wickedness of human beings in the *kaliyuga* that only rarely is one so filled with love of God as to become a fit receptacle for divine favour, which is thus hard to obtain (*durlabha*) rather than easy (*sulabha*).[15] But a person must not give up endeavour and prayer. Dumont has called *bhakti* 'a

[15] Cf.: 'Viewed from man's side, Ramanuja holds, the attainment of God is anything but easy, for it implies the very difficult achievement of perfectly disciplined meditation on God. Even more important is the fact that this intimate communion with God is not something that man can gain: not even the advanced devotee who yearns desperately for this communion can gain it by his own effort. Salvation is God's election and God's gift' (Carman 1974: 85).

The emergence of strong Vaishnava influences among the Shaivite Kashmiri Brahmans is another important development in the cultural history of Kashmir that awaits careful research.

revolutionary doctrine since it transcends both caste and renunciation, and opens for all without distinction an easy road to salvation' (1960: 57). It is interesting to note how the Pandits have retained the idea of *bhakti* as an 'easy road' and yet managed to emphasize that it is hard to reach and tread it. Failure is necessarily that of the seeker, not of the 'path'.

Now, the longing for divine love and grace does not require one to abandon one's family and become a renouncer. It so transforms and enlarges one's affections as to make them all partake of divine love. The love of God is not exclusive and does not require withdrawal. As many informants put it, '*bhakti* does not drain the heart but fills it evermore with love'. That is, *bhakti* requires that the love of one's kith and kin should be encompassed by and not independent of the love of God. The devotee does not fall into the snare of rituals either, for divine love is an attitude of life. Rituals have their place in a person's life, for they help to maintain *bhaṭṭil*, but rituals are only a means to the end. The devotee learns to be detached in the midst of involvement, concentrating on the only true attachment, that to the divinity. He knows himself to be alone or isolated (*keval*), though he has a family, and seeks perfection through union with the unique (*kaivalya*), that is, the divinity. His attitude is one of utter humility and submission to God. In the course of my fieldwork I have met a few people of whom others said that they were men of God and led 'pure lives', though they were householders with wives and children.[16]

Śakti

Kashmir has another celebrated tradition, namely that of the quest for inner illumination (*prakāśa*) through the pursuit of occult power (*śakti*) (see, e.g., Woodroffe 1978). This is the domain of *tantra*, a body of sophisticated technical knowledge, and ordinary householders of the kind I have worked with

[16] There is a category of exceptional people who should be mentioned here. To all intents and purposes they are mad or deranged and found among the Pandits as well as the Muslims. The Kashmiris, however, consider them as people 'touched by God' (to quote an informant), for they are said to be clairvoyant and gifted with the capacity to bless and curse. They do not acknowledge family ties or observe the rules of social intercourse. It is interesting how such persons, irrespective of their Pandit or Muslim birth, serve as a link between the two communities.

have only vague or confused ideas about it. Over the years I have met only one Pandit who described himself to me as a novitiate *śākta* (one in pursuit of *śakti*), but have been told of a few others, dead or alive, who were or are adepts.

According to popular belief, the *śākta* seeks, through *kriyā*—consisting of study, discussion, reflection, ritual and yoga—the arousal of *śakti*, which resides in every human being, but lies dormant, coiled like a somnolent snake (*kuṇḍalinī*) at the bottom of the spine. It can be aroused, however, and raised to the head and enable the seeker to realize his own divinity, his oneness with Shiva. I have heard stories of the miraculous powers of the *śākta*, of how they can even control the processes of nature, such as seasons and earthquakes. I have also been told that the ordinary rules of *bhaṭṭil* do not bind a *śākta*; thus he may eat meat in places and on occasions when the ordinary Pandit dare not do so and also transgress other norms of the householder's life. Though some tantric texts speak of the *pañcatattva* (the sacramental consumption of mutton, fish and alcohol, sexual intercourse, and the employment of bodily postures) for the attainment of *śakti*, my informants denied that sexuality had any special place whatsoever in a *śākta*'s life.

According to my informants, there can be no personal family for a *śākta* but he may live in an exclusive household of his own, consisting of his family members. Preferably he may live with his preceptor (*guru*) and fellow-seekers, and at a later stage have his own disciples (*śiṣya*) to minister to his needs. One of these may be adopted as a son so that funeral and post-mortuary rites can be performed. The *śākta* is thus not exactly a man without a household, though he is different from ordinary householders. His way of life is certainly more than a mere re-orientation: it is an alternative way of life, though defined in relation to a householder. In fact, most of his disciples are householders who seek light from him and his blessings, without themselves abandoning their families and other worldly pursuits. The *śākta* looms on the horizon of the Pandit's cultural universe. That the Brahmans of Kashmir were once renowned Shaivites and Shaktins who made outstanding contributions to the philosophy and practice of *tantra* is now only a very dim memory in the lives of the villagers I have lived with.

Virakti

I have mentioned above the Pandit attitude to renunciation. In the course of my inquiries I encountered no renouncers, strictly defined, among the Pandits: such sannyasis as one does encounter in Kashmir are usually non-Kashmiris. Some individuals, mostly men, may live away from home but they do not go through formal initiation into any sannyasi order. There is also no emphasis at all upon the termination of the *gṛhastha āśrama* (the stage of the householder) in one's life. As a person grows older, he is expected to become increasingly God-centred, but no one is expected to live away from home. In this sense, formal renunciation is not merely postponed, as Dumont (1960: 45) points out, but its place in the life of the Pandit is denied. There are only two stages of life: that of the child who lives with his parents, and that of the adult who has his children living with him. Both stages are phases in the life of the householder. The *gṛhastha* sustains the world: to recall, he is the *duniyā-dār*.[17] If he succeeds in cultivating detachment from the passions (*virakti*), that should be enough but even that is not easy.

The attitude of Pandits towards those who make claims of detachment, and particularly of renunciation, is generally one of scepticism. Individual men and women may command respect, and even a following, but most of them are dismissed as charlatans. The general term of reference for such persons is *sādh* (from the Sanskrit *sādhu*) and it is related to and rhymed with *bād*, flatus (from the Persian word for air), in lighthearted banter. In a similar vein, an old saying warns the Pandit against the company of the renouncers as they will make him give his wife (and household) and never make him privy to their esoteric secrets!

In view of their almost total absence among them, why is it that the Pandits distrust and ridicule self-styled renouncers? I do not think that the answer lies in the Pandits' having a higher standard than other Hindu communities by which to judge such claims; it lies rather in their commitment to the

[17] Cf. Manusmriti (III.78): 'Because men of the three other orders are daily supported by the householder with (gifts of) sacred knowledge and food, therefore, (the order of) householders is the most excellent order' (Bühler 1964: 89).

ideology of the householder. Apparently they are cynical about those who leave home because most such people never had families of their own (either because they were unable to get married or because they became widowed before becoming fathers) or their relations with their kin have been strained.

At a deeper level, however, one might detect a fear of the renouncer, for he poses a threat to the ideology of the householder and plenitude. Unlike the former, he not only seeks release from the web of kinship and other worldly ties but also denigrates these as a trap and an illusion. The renouncer is too powerful an adversary to be contemplated with equanimity. Individual renouncers are usually accorded respect in face-to-face encounters; they are fed and offered gifts. When talking about them generally, however, they are ridiculed and even reviled and their genuineness is generally doubted. Dumont (1960: 45) is quite right in speaking of 'subdued hostility' towards renunciation. In fact, the Pandits reduce the renouncer to a caricature of his ideal self; that the caricature is only too often an accurate enough portrait of the 'holy men' one actually meets is another matter but not totally irrelevant. The real point seems to be that only when the renouncer is thus portrayed may he be convincingly employed as a foil to highlight the virtues of the life of the householder: these are said to flow from 'detachment in enjoyment' which is the essence of renunciation.[18] An informant once went into the details of the way of life of the mythological Janaka to emphasize that Janaka was not only the *king* of Mithila but also a great *householder*, and, at the same time, the supreme *renouncer*.

CONCLUDING REMARKS

The Pandits' ideology of the householder is, in fact, much more than just that: it is their ideology of humanity. While all sentient beings are born (and die), human beings are 'made' or

[18] At a Pandit wedding I observed in 1983 (after this essay had been first published), the priest explained to the bridegroom the significance of the *kanyādāna* thus: 'The maiden is gifted to you by her father for the purpose of *dharma*, *artha*, *kāma*, and *mokṣa*. Now, *dharma* is not putting the *tyok* mark on one's forehead: it consists of discharging one's debts to gods, gurus, and ancestors. *Artha* is the making of money and *kāma* the pursuit of luxuries (sic). The ideal is not renunciation but

constructed through the *saṁskāra* and achieve different degrees of perfection by their conduct. A boy attains the full ritual and moral status of a Pandit when he receives the girdle and the holy neck cord. In the case of girls, it is marriage which bestows such status. Marriage is crucial for men as well as women, for then alone do they become true householders. Bachelors, widowers and widows are members of households but not *gṛhastha* themselves and are, therefore, regarded as unfortunate. The greatest ambition of a male Pandit is to become a householder along with his own wife and children.

Children and women

The ideology is, however, almost silent on children and women: they come in only indirectly—in relation to men. This is, perhaps, partly because as a man I have not had the same free access to women informants in the course of my fieldwork as to men, but the main reason lies deeper—in the ideology itself, in Pandit culture. As I have described elsewhere (1965), the Pandits greatly desire and value children, particularly sons. In fact, to be a *gṛhastha* is to be a parent and this is why the bachelor and the childless widow are pitied much more than a widower or a widow who does have children. Children, of course, have a most important place in the emotional lives of adults but they acquire a structural significance only when they themselves become adults. In fact, it is not children or adults who are important but *bhaṭṭil*.

Children acquire the Pandit identity initially by the fact of being born to Pandit parents. Their conduct is regulated under the guidance of adults till they are sufficiently grown up to act independently. Many concessions are made in their favour and lapses from proper conduct condoned, but once a boy has gone through his ritual initiation, and a girl has been married, the full range of the expectations and constraints that constitute *bhaṭṭil* becomes applicable. Prior to these events boys and girls do not have the ritual status of adults. This fact is dramatized in their being neither entitled to full cremation rites and

householdership. Having done all this one must seek refuge in God: that is *mokṣa*.' I later checked the text of the marriage ritual (according to Laugākṣa) that the priest had been following: it did not mention *mokṣa* at all.

post-mortuary food offerings, nor susceptible to ritual pollution by births and deaths in the circle of kinsfolk. The absence of children in the ideology is, therefore, not an absence at all: it is an anticipation of adulthood. The child is the adult in making.

The absence of a well-articulated place for women in the ideology is a more complex matter and calls for clarification, particularly because every Pandit woman is a married householder and even the idea of a woman renouncer is absent.[19] There is a sense in which the Pandit women—they are called *Bhaṭṭani*—are a 'muted group' seen in the light of a dominant male system of perception (Ardener 1977). The men recognize that in the reality of everyday life women are very important: 'What is a home without the *gharavājin* (mistress)?' they ask.[20] A married woman is also called a '*gṛhasthadārin*', the bearer of the burden of *gārhasthya*. A man works out his destiny as a human being and a Pandit in the company of the domestic 'others' who include women, notably his mother and wife. In his ritual performances—a major *pūjā*, a life cycle ritual, a *śrāddha*—the presence of the wife is essential.

If all this be so, why do women remain 'muted' in the ideology? An answer to this question formulated by my male informants was that *bhaṭṭil* is as much a concern of women as it is of men, but in the domain of domestic activity, women's work is in the kitchen—which is their specific responsibility—and their participation in rituals is moderately or severely restricted during the duration of menstruation. A menstruating woman must particularly exclude herself completely from rituals for the dead or else they lose all their efficacy. Similarly, a woman polluted by menses may not enter the *pūjā* room in the house or a temple and in no case make offerings to the deities. She may, however, say her prayers and even circumambulate a sacred place.

[19] There is, of course, the celebrated fourteenth century Shaivite mystic Lalla (or Lal Ded) who abandoned home and became a wanderer and whose sayings (*vākya*) are a living part of the Pandit oral tradition. She, however, represents the proverbial exception that proves the rule, for Lalla was no ordinary woman (see Kaul 1973).

[20] Cf. Rig Veda III.53.4: 'the wife herself is the home'.

Apart from the limitation which is seen to arise from the physical–moral nature (*zāt*) of the women, there are other conventions which establish the superiority of men. Thus a woman does not offer water or food to manes; she does not have the authority to invest her son with the girdle and the holy neck cord: if his father is not available, the proper surrogate for the absentee parent is an agnatic kinsman; nor, indeed, does a woman give her daughter away in marriage. And yet (as stated above) she is present by her husband's side on all such major occasions: she is defined in relation to him. It is a hierarchical relation and proclaims their unity which is, however, complex in the sense that man encompasses and is superior to woman.

The most concrete expression of the foregoing fact is that, from the day of his marriage, a man wears a holy neck cord of six instead of three strands of cotton, each set of three symbolizing his responsibility to discharge the debts (*ṛṇa*) towards gods, gurus and ancestors—one on his own behalf and the other on behalf of his wife. But as Dumont (on whose work the foregoing formulation is based) has rightly pointed out,

> The same hierarchical principle that in some way subordinates one level to another at the same time introduces a multiplicity of levels, letting the situation reverse itself. The mother of the family (an Indian family, for example) inferior though she may be made by her sex [I would like to say sex *and* gender or physiology *and* ideology] in some respects nonetheless dominates the relationships within the family (1980: 241).

In short, the ideology places different values on men and women and thus generates an idiom which includes reference to women when men are spoken of. The relative position of men and women is given in their relationship. Needless to add, the reality of everyday life does not wholly follow the ideology in its full detail: to assert this would amount to suggesting the false and suppressing the ethnographic truth.

The man-in-the-world

The ideology of everyday life, then, clearly establishes the Pandit as the *gṛhastha*. The householder is the man-in-world.

The house he lives in is, in fact, the microcosm of the earth and its presiding deity (*gharadevatā*) is none other than Vastoshpati, the protector of the earth. Such a person's prime concern is with the maturation of his self (person), which is ensured if he organizes his life in strict conformity with traditional purposes, employing appropriate procedures for their achievement. Release from the chain of transmigration is frankly admitted to be a very distant goal, and, therefore, one concentrates in the meanwhile on the slow but steady accumulation of merit by the conscious effort to lead a disciplined life.

As a householder, a Pandit may legitimately seek plenitude and joy but only if this endeavour is controlled by *dharma*. As a sensitive informant once put it to me, 'to lead the life of a householder is like seeking to warm oneself by fire—one might also get burnt by it.' In other words, while the life of the householder is the source of joy, it also brings sorrow and, if one deviates from the path of *dharma*, it could also lead the way to perdition. To quote further from the same informant: 'The home is the place neither for the indulgence of one's physical appetites (*bhogaśālā*) nor for the performance of austerities (*yogaśālā*).' It is the narrow middle ground, the 'razor's edge': 'Like the sharp edge of a razor is the path, narrow and difficult to tread' (Katha Upanishad I.iii.14).

The Pandit seeks meritorious fulfilment in life through the affirmation of family and wider kinship obligations and through the willing acceptance of other social bonds which result from the pursuits of generally accepted worldly goals (*artha*). These bonds include his relations with the non-Pandits also. He wants success in the work he does, and cares for being thought of well in his village as much as he wants to lead a happy domestic life. There is thus a continuity in the Pandit's life between the domestic and the extra-domestic domains and between what may be called the religious and secular spheres, just as there is a continuity between the home and the earth itself.

Bhaṭṭil is a total view of life which excludes nothing but it is a hierarchical view of both the ultimate purposes of life and the tasks of everyday existence. Discrimination rather than withdrawal is the watchword of the Pandit's life. He is, however, expected to remain always mindful that there is something higher than good *karma* and this is divine grace. The path of occult power or renunciation is for the selected few. For the common Pandit, the life of the man-in-the-world—epitomized in the role of the householder—though arduous, is the moral and good life. It is a life worth living.[21]

[21] After this book had gone to the printer, I came across an essay on Kashmiri Brahmans based on Sanskrit texts of the medieval period (9th–13th centuries). What I find remarkable are the continuities between the ideas of those times and of the present-day Pandits, the intervening centuries and the disruptions resulting from the Muslim incursion notwithstanding. Thus, we read: 'The Brahmanism of the middle ground . . . offered the Brahman householder a monism for the ritual agent which admitted renunciation but tended to confine it to the last quarter of a man's life (after the payment of the three debts), and at the same time made it an unnecessary option by propagating a doctrine of gnostic liberation within the pursuit of conformity to the householder's dharma' (Sanderson 1985: 197). The householder 'was to perfect himself through disinterested conformity to God's will manifest as his dharma' (ibid.: 198).

2
AUSPICIOUSNESS AND PURITY

> There are many auspicious and inauspicious moments in one's life, just as there are in a day. The most auspicious moment of the day is the rising of the sun. It fills the earth, the sky and the heavens with light and brings with it the promise of good works and wisdom for men. It is like the birth of a son—the most auspicious moment in a man's life—but while childbirth pollutes the very same people, namely the parents, whom it makes most happy, sunrise manifests the glory of God, enlivens our intelligence, and purifies the whole earth.
>
> A KASHMIRI PANDIT

INTRODUCTORY

During the last three decades or so the sociology of South Asian societies has been characterized by a deepening concern with the people's categories of thought over and above the attention that has long been given to the study of social organization. This is a welcome development inasmuch as people everywhere not only engage in social behaviour but also have *ideas* about the motivations and justifications of their actions. In other words, what they do is meaningful to themselves and it is only proper that the sociologist should concern himself equally with rule-governed behaviour *and* with its significance to the actors.

Thus, the work of many scholars, including Louis Dumont and M. N. Srinivas, has contributed significantly to the examination of certain ideas underlying characteristic forms of behaviour in Hindu society, notably the ideas of 'purity' and 'pollution'. There are other cognitive structures which await exploration in the context of the inter-relatedness of ideology and actual behaviour. In recent years the notion of 'auspiciousness' in the senses of benediction and well-being, enveloping the everyday life of ordinary people at the one end and of extraordinary personages such as the king at the other, has emerged as one such concern of central importance in the study of Hindu, Buddhist and Jaina cultures (see, for example, Carman and Marglin 1985). In fact, in traditional Indian thought one of the auspicious events in the life of common people was sight of the king—so much so, indeed, that the later Muslim kings of India, the great Moghuls, yielded to the popular demand of blessing people by allowing themselves to be seen by morning crowds gathered outside the royal fort, even though this was against the spirit of Islam.

In this chapter I am concerned with an attempt to clarify the notion of 'auspiciousness' and to examine its relation to 'purity' by exploring some of their meanings in Hindu or, more precisely, Brahmanical culture.[1] The published ethnographic studies on 'auspiciousness' are by no means as rich as those on 'purity' and they are certainly less clear even than those on the latter subject. The present exercise is, therefore (to borrow T. S. Eliot's words), 'a raid on the inarticulate' and that too 'with shabby equipment'. I make the attempt, nevertheless; while doing so I use deliberately, but only as far as seems reasonable, the Sanskrit words *śubha* and *śuddha* instead of 'aus-

[1] R. S. Khare has raised the question as to whether the idea of auspiciousness is, like ritual purity, 'a monopoly of the twice-born' (1976a: 121n). Louis Dumont in a comment on an earlier draft of the present essay wrote that the Kallar of Tamilnadu, the subcaste of which he made an intensive study, are little concerned with astrological matters; he suggested that auspiciousness is a brahmanical idea, implying that it is not of the same general importance as purity and pollution. G. S. Bhatt, who has devoted many years to the study of Scheduled Castes, such as the Chamar in Uttar Pradesh, informs me that low castes do have beliefs regarding auspiciousness/inauspiciousness and consult astrologers on such matters as the performance of life-cycle rituals. This perhaps points to the deeper inroads of the ideas and behaviour of upper castes in the lives of lower castes in north India than in south India.

Bh. Krishnamurthy, who also read an earlier draft of this essay, writes (in a personal communication): 'Most of the practices and beliefs described in the article have counterparts in the Dravidian languages area. It would be interesting to sort out how many of these had their origin in the native (folk) cultures of India cutting across the caste system and how many are prevalent only in the higher castes. I am thinking of, for example, *śubhanakṣtra*, which is a part of the religious observances of upper castes as opposed to *śubha śakuna*, which is prevalent in many communities including tribals.' It is obvious that we need more ethnographic data on this subject than we have now to answer these (and other) questions.

piciousness' and 'purity'. The former two words or derivatives from the same are in use in most languages of India. My hesitation in using the two English words throughout the chapter arises from the fact that they have become omnibus words and conceal more than they reveal, and this might vitiate my attempt to clarify the significance of the Hindu concepts under consideration.[2] Moreover, and more importantly, my approach to the problem makes it imperative that words actually employed in everyday speech be examined in the context of their use. Without entering into philosophical controversies or invoking the technical literature on semantics, I would like to maintain that we can learn a great deal about the meaning or meanings of a family of words by examining them in the contexts of other meanings (which is what 'use' really is). It seems to me permissible to do so for my limited purpose without going into the question of whether abstract meanings exist or not.

ON THE CATEGORIES OF 'ŚUBHA' AND 'ŚUDDHA': NOTES ON EVERYDAY USAGE[3]

The everyday (ordinary language) use of the word *śubha* refers most frequently and directly to time and to temporal events in

[2] To elaborate this point, the Fathers at the Delhi Jesuit seminary Vidyajyoti assured me during a discussion (in 1980) that the word 'auspiciousness' has no standard use in their language other than in reference to the 'superstitions' of pre-Christian European peoples and of non-Christians generally. No comment is necessary. As for 'purity', I know from my fieldwork in the Kashmir Valley that the brahmanical notion of *śuddha* and the Muslim idea of *pāk*, both rendered into English as 'pure' or 'purity', for no other appropriate words seem to be available, differ significantly in their connotation. Thus, *pāk* cooked food of the Muslim is totally unacceptable to the Brahman because it is incurably polluting. Similarly, no good Muslim eats food which has come out of a Hindu kitchen; it is simply *harām*, forbidden.

A disclaimer is perhaps called for immediately, lest I should be misunderstood to be retreating behind a curtain of Sanskrit words (or words from other Indian languages) into a naïve cultural relativism. I remember Goethe's admonition that, so long as we know no foreign language, we are in a sense ignorant of our own. Comparison is, indeed, the foundation on which anthropology—our knowledge, understanding and evaluation of human cultures through mutual interpretation—is based. In short, all I am trying to do is to argue that direct (surface) translation from one language to another, far from contributing to our general understanding of cultural constructs, in fact often hinders them.

[3] The data for this paper are drawn from the following main sources: (i) My

relation to particular categories of people. Thus the word *śubha* —or its opposite *aśubha*—is prefixed to nouns such as *samaya* or *kāla* (time) for the performance of a particular significant act which is a joyous event in itself or is expected to have happy consequences. A time which may be considered auspicious for one kind of actions may not, however, be so for another: while the night is auspicious for the worship of Mahakali, it is not so for the worship of Vishnu. Similarly, *śubha* is used along with such words as *avasara* (occasion), *utsava* (festival), *ṛtu* (season), *māsa* (month), *divasa* (day), *ghaḍi* and *kṣaṇa* (a moment or measure of time). More specifically, *śubha* qualifies *muhūrta* (astrologically appropriate moment for doing something significant) and *lagna* (the moment of the sun's entry into a zodiacal space or sign). Contextually, people speak of *ārambha* (beginning), *anta* (ending), *samāpana* (completion), *āgamana* (coming), *gamana* (going), *yātrā* (pilgrimage), etc. as *śubha*, invoking benediction by doing so. *Śubha* is also employed to refer to happy events (for example, *janma*, birth, or *vivāha*, marriage) and information about them (*sūcanā*, *samācāra*), to signs (*saṅketa*), omens (*śakuna*), etc. *Śubhakārya* and *śubhācāra* respectively refer to any specific act or conduct generally which is conducive to well-being. To ensure such well-being through success and happy consequences in any kind of work, ranging from the routine to the extraordinary, people consult astrologers, priests or almanacs to find out the auspicious moment or time for—to give a few examples—wearing a new garment, buying provisions, starting on a journey, or performing a ritual. Negatively, when unfortunate events which it is feared might occur do not occur or, having occurred, do not result in major misfortune, auspiciousness is said to have prevailed. The agency which ensures this well-being may be divine grace, the configuration of circumstances and/or human effort.

In all the foregoing uses of the prefix *śubha*, the focus is on the directional flow of time—on temporal sequences and critical points in them—rather than on time as such. The passage of

---

efforts, now extended over many years, to interpret various aspects of the way of life of Kashmiri Brahmans by interrogation and observation (including field-work in a village); (ii) recent conversations with several Uttar Pradeshi (Chaturvedi, Kanyakubja and Saryupari) Brahmans of Kanpur and Lucknow on the specific theme of this paper; (iii) a few selected ethnographic works.

time becomes significant through the conjunction or intersection of the trajectories of human lives and/or of such trajectories and the course of cosmic forces.

The evidence of everyday speech indicates that the notion of auspiciousness is also associated with places, objects and persons connected with the kind of events or actions mentioned above. An altar set up or a place marked out for a ritual performance is called a *śubha-sthali* or *sthāna*. Once the ceremony is over the altar may be demolished and the sacred area earlier set apart reverts to its daily routine uses. The kitchen (*cauka*) and the room reserved for daily worship (*pūjā-kakṣa*) are particularly auspicious places in a house so long as it is inhabited. A celestial *śubha* space which is much talked about is the *nakṣatra* (a constellation through which the moon passes at a particular time: a lunar mansion). Certain directions (*diśā*) and cardinal points in space are also regarded as *śubha* or *aśubha*. Thus, facing the east while performing a ritual is regarded as desirable through its association with sunrise, and facing the south is regarded as undesirable through its association with death.

A *tīrthasthāna*, or place of pilgrimage, located on the bank of a river or a body of water, is regarded as holy and a pilgrimage (*yātrā*) to it is auspicious. The holiness of the place and the auspiciousness of the visit are greatly enhanced if two or more rivers merge there: it is then elevated to the status of *saṅgama*, that is, the place from where two or more streams flow together.[4] One of India's most holy place of pilgrimage—the *tīrtharāja*, or the king of places of pilgrimage—is Prayag (in Uttar Pradesh) where the holy rivers Ganga and Yamuna and the subterranean Sarasvati meet and where the famous twelve-yearly bathing festival of *kumbha* is held whenever a particular astrological conjunction (*yoga*), namely Jupiter in aries, occurs. The focus is on movement, which is what *yātrā* denotes, and on 'crossing over', or 'reaching forward', from a less to a more desirable state of being, achieved by a ritual bathing in the holy waters, which is what *tīrtha* signifies: in the words of a Kashmiri Brahman informant, 'more than the impurities of

[4] It is worth noting here that one of the secondary meanings of the word *saṅgama* is sexual union, which is thus regarded as being comparable to the merger of rivers and is similarly auspicious.

the outer body (*tana*), it is the impurities of the mind (*mana*) that are thus washed away'. As in the case of time, it is not a place as such but what can possibly happen there to certain categories of people that marks it out as auspicious: we are once again confronted with the notion of intersection of the trajectories of cosmic forces, symbolized by moving planets and flowing rivers, and human lives.

Besides points in time and space, certain objects also are considered auspicious. The most notable example is the *kalaśa*, a metal (gold, silver, copper or brass) or earthen vessel containing water from a river (or rivers) and other auspicious substances such as dry fruits.[5] The Kashmiri Brahmans treat it as a representation of Ganesha, the deity who removes obstacles (*vighnahartā*) and bestows success on the works of human beings (*siddhidātā*) and thus symbolizes auspiciousness. The *kalaśa* is associated with the *commencement* of a ritual, when it is consecrated and worshipped, and with its *completion* when its contents are distributed by sprinkling worshippers with the water and, to cite the practice of Kashmiri Brahmans again, offering them the walnuts, earlier placed in the vessel, to eat: doing so is considered to be conducive to well-being.

The adjective *śubha* is applied in everyday speech to actors (*kartā*) when they are seen performing actions which are conducive to joy and well-being (*śubhakārya*) or when they symbolize these states. For instance, and crucially, a *śubhacintaka* (well-wisher) is one who entertains good thoughts about another's influence on the course of the latter's life. One who conveys good news is called *śubhasūcanī*. A specific usage among the upper castes in the Hindi-speech areas worth mentioning here is the reference to prostitutes as *maṅgalamukhī*, that is, one whose face produces well-being when seen. The distinction between the state of auspiciousness and the creative agent (*maṅgalakāraka* or *kalyāṇakāraka*) is most important, as is the relation between

[5] As is well known to students of classical texts, the contents of the *kalaśa* vary with the occasion. Thus, the contents of the vessel at the coronation ceremony of Hindu kings included the water of many rivers, earth from many places and dwellings, jewels, medicinal herbs, etc. 'The *pūrṇa kumbha* (*kalaśa*, *ghaṭa*) is, minimally, a pot filled with water, with green leaves from fruit-bearing trees, especially mango leaves, covering its mouth, and a coconut placed on top. The pot, placed on white raw rice, is the most widely used sign of auspiciousness (*maṅgala*, *śubha*)' (Marglin 1982: 161).

the two (the signification). The point to note about these usages and similar others is that it is not the person himself or herself who is auspicious, but rather his or her intentions, actions, or even merely the presence (and witnessing the same), which are so and are, therefore, expected to have happy consequences. The ultimate source of auspiciousness is, of course, the divinity (cf. Carman 1974: 172, 255).

A crucial contribution to the explication of the significance of the category *śubha* comes from the speech of priests and astrologers, which is an element in the conversation of those who consult these specialists. Such people believe that their lives are subject to the influence of the nine *grahas*, headed by *sūrya* (Sun) and including *bṛhaspati*, *budha*, *candramā*, *ketu*, *maṅgala*, *rāhu*, *śanaiścara* and *śukra* (corresponding to Jupiter, Mercury, Moon, Dragon's Tail, Mars, Dragon's Head, Saturn and Venus). These *grahas* are classified into two categories, namely *śubha* (beneficent) and *aśubha* or *krūra* (cruel, fierce, formidable, maleficent). Only three of these—*bṛhaspati*, *candramā*, *śukra*—were described to me by my Kashmiri Brahman informants as being *śubha*; *budha* is considered 'impotent' or neutral and the rest fierce. It does not, however, really matter very much to a human being what the nature of a *graha* is, except in so far as any one of them, or any combination of them (*yoga*), comes to have a dominant influence on the course of his life trajectory as a result of the aspect of these heavenly beings. This fact of astral influence is called *daśā*, that is the condition and fate of a human being as affected by the movement of a *graha*. These planetary movements affect the lives of people variously, depending primarily upon the time (*kāla*) and place (*sthāna*) of their birth. Thus even a maleficent *graha* may bring joy, health and prosperity to an individual owing to its location in a particular place (*gṛha*) in his birth-time horoscope (*janmakuṇḍalī*) and/or the horoscope for the year (*varṣakuṇḍalī*) and the relation of this location to the *graha*'s own position during a particular period of time; zodiacal spaces are classified in respect of each *graha* as his own, his friends' or his enemies' 'homes'. In this regard, the critical datum of every individual horoscope is the *lagna*, that is, the zodiacal sign under which one is born: starting from there, the life trajectory of the individual can be charted, which is what the casting or writing of a horoscope involves. The auspiciousness or inauspiciousness of a life trajectory is stated in degrees rather than in absolute terms. An individual is thus conceptualized as a *pātra* ('vessel') to be filled.

Now, childbirth, particularly the birth of a son, is normally an auspicious event, but it may not always be so. The configuration of *graha* and *nakṣatra* at the time of his birth may make a particular son a menace to the well-being of his parents and, therefore, his birth is considered to be an inauspicious event. In other words, the influence of his life trajectory on those of his parents may turn out to be maleficent, reinforcing the unfortunate elements of their own trajectories and weakening the beneficent ones. For example, a boy born on the *mūla nakṣatra* to a Kashmiri Brahman family is adjudged to be a potential parricide, not of course by a wilful act of future murder but by virtue of the subtle influence of one life's trajectory on the other. Nobody else would accept such a child in adoption. To avert the mortal threat, he may be abandoned near the entrance of a temple, or some such holy place, thus being entrusted to the care of gods. In fact, this act may be seen as one of symbolic destruction. The family priest then picks up the child—the whole act is of course pre-arranged—and exchanges him for money and grain with the child's own family with a member of which he has a 'chance' encounter.

Such happenings are not common, but Hindus generally perform rituals regularly in an effort to ward off or at least minimize the dangers posed by inauspicious births or unfavourable *daśā*. These rituals are called *upāya* or 'corrective' actions. The most notable of these rituals that has come to my notice is *tulābhāra*, when the body of the endangered person is symbolically replaced by weighing him against grain, pulses and other prescribed substances which are then given away to the family priest.[6] The body is reconstituted by means of a ritual bath, which involves its being washed with clays, herbs, water, etc.

[6] The fact that priests accept 'ominous children' and 'dangerous goods' from their patrons (*yajamāna*) testifies to the belief in their superior capacity to cope with dangerous situations. They thus come to symbolize danger itself. At the same time there is, at least among Kashmiri Brahmans, a barely concealed deprecation of priests for the same reasons and, hence, a sense of inauspiciousness is aroused on encountering them on particular occasions (when, for instance, their services are not required).

from various places. Expectedly, the whole series of rites is regarded as highly hazardous to the subject, though their purpose is to stave off the ultimate danger of death.

The extent to which such rituals succeed in warding off evil is not wholly predictable, for auspiciousness can neither be totally engineered nor inauspiciousness wholly averted, no matter what promotive or corrective steps may be taken. It was pointed out to me by a Chaturvedi Brahman informant that, though the marriage of Rama was performed at an auspicious time and the appointed time for his consecration as the king was similarly calculated, his married life was interrupted (because of the abduction of Sita by Ravana) and finally ended in sorrow (when Sita immolated herself); similarly his becoming king was postponed by his fourteen years' exile.

Birth is normally a *śubha* event and death is *aśubha*. Yet the degree and nature of inauspiciousness of death also are determined by the time and place at which it occurs and by other related circumstances. There is a recurrent inauspicious period in every month of the lunar calendar called *pañcaka*, when five *nakṣatras* are in conjunction, for the duration of which the performance of many actions is forbidden as far as possible. The cremation of a dead body during *pañcaka* is considered very unfortunate but cannot be avoided. It was explained to me that the occurrence of death during such a period is replete with dangers for the journey of the dead or departed person (*preta*) into *pitṛloka* (the abode of the manes) and is also inauspicious for the survivors, five of whom may die in the ensuing year.

Death is inauspicious, but widowhood is an even more unfortunate event for an upper caste Hindu woman. It brings about a drastic change in her social identity and ritual status (see Madan 1975a). Among the Kashmiri Brahmans, when an old woman dies and her husband, older than her, accompanies the funeral party to the cremation ground, many women loudly express the wish that they too may die the same way, survived by the husband and sons.

Let me now turn to a more complex set of usages which may not appear to be covered by the foregoing analysis. The example that comes most readily to mind is the widespread practice among Hindi-speaking people of using the expression *śubhanāma* (rendered as 'good name' in Indian English) when inquiring about each other's names.[7] Similarly, a person's body or parts of it, for example the face or palms of the hands, may be said to bear *śubhalakṣaṇa* (auspicious signs or marks). While it would be appropriate to point out that the word *śubha* here refers to loveliness, grace, splendour, lustrousness, etc. (see Monier-Williams 1976), it must also be noted that these qualities are not so much values as signs indicative of the future course of events in an individual's life and his influence on the lives of others.[8] Kashmiri Brahmans extol Shiva as the most benign and beneficent divinity, for (to quote from a popular hymn) 'he is the one with all the *śubhalakṣaṇa*'.

To highlight the proper usage of the word *śubha*, it may be pointed out finally that there are certain human actions which create well-being through the very fact of being performed, so that one does not have to await an auspicious time for their performance or for their consequences. The Kashmiri Brahmans, who do not normally undertake a journey away from home except at an auspicious moment, do not consider it equally necessary to time similarly the return home, which is always auspicious. Similarly, whatever is done daily, including *pūjā*, and the cooking of food, does not have to await an auspicious hour though it has to be done outside a particularly inauspicious time, such as the duration of an eclipse or the presence of a dead body in the house. Some informants from Uttar Pradesh pointed to a further distinction in this regard, namely, that between *vyavahārika* (conventional) and *ādhyātmika* or *paramārthika* (spiritual) actions: when an action is motivated spiritually and not undertaken merely as a matter of convention or routine, the constraint of an inauspicious period of time—such as eclipses, *malamāsa* or *devaśayana*—becomes inoperative.[9]

[7] Bh. Krishnamurthy comments (in a personal communication): '*Śubhanāma* seems to be a recent innovation. There is no corresponding expression in the Southern languages; and there is no antonym, *aśubhanāma*.'

[8] According to a Chaturvedi Brahman informant, applying the *tilaka* (a very visible mark of auspiciousness) on the forehead produces well-being, particularly if this is done with the thumb of the right hand (the Kashmiri Brahmans use the middle finger) and if the thumb has *śubhalakṣaṇa* on it.

[9] The distinction between *ādhyātmika* or *paramārthika* and *vyavahārika* was made by some Uttar Pradeshi informants, as also by R. S. Khare (in a personal communication) who has written extensively on the Kanyakubja Brahmans (see Khare 1976a and 1976b).

The foregoing selection from a thesaurus of usages (collected by me in Kashmir and Uttar Pradesh) points to the conclusion that the 'family resemblance' which obtains among them has its roots in the significance of the *passage of time* for human beings, which varies from one category of persons to another and even from one individual to another. What is crucial is not an abstract conception of time *per se*—which is neutral in character—but the intersection of cosmic and individual life trajectories which this flux entails. Auspiciousness, then, is an absolute value which manifests as a quality of events in the lives of human actors (*pātra*) and involves the dimensions of time (*kāla*) and space (*sthāna*).

The word *śuddha*, in contrast to *śubha*, is not generally used in everyday speech to refer to events.[10] The connotation of this word is conveyed by invoking images of fulness or completeness in the specific sense of perfection. It thus refers to the most desired condition of the human body or, more comprehensively, the most desired state of being. *Śuddha* and its opposite *aśuddha* are attributes of animate beings, inanimate objects and places with which a human being comes into contact in the course of everyday life. For example, a prepubescent unmarried girl (*kanyā*), water from a holy river, unboiled milk, ghee and a temple are *śuddha*. On the other hand, contact with certain kinds of human beings (low-caste Hindus or non-Hindus), animals (dogs), objects (goods made of leather), foods (beef or food cooked in impure utensils), substances (discharges from a human body), places (cremation ground), etc. causes Brahmans and other upper-caste Hindus to become polluted. The notion

[10] A Saryupari Brahman informant, who is a pundit and an astrologer, told me that he would not hesitate to speak of a *śuddha* moment of time from the point of view of the natural occurrence of an event or of a performance. Commenting on this, Baidyanath Saraswati writes (in a personal communication): 'Based on astrological calculation, a particular period, ranging from five to ten days or so, is called *śuddha* when the famous "marriage mart" of the Maithil Brahmans takes place (in Bihar) and marriages are solemnized. Within that period there are, of course, specific moments of time that are considered *śubha* for the ceremony. The duration of the *aśuddha* period from the point of view of marriage—called *aticara*—could be very much longer, lasting two to three years.'

In this connection, one informant pointed out that the horoscope of the Buddha contained the perfect conjunction (*yoga*) of *graha* and thus the *purity* of his Being also embodied the *auspiciousness* of Time.

of perfection in the sense of freedom from error or fault is extended to certain actions also, as exemplified by such expressions as *śuddha-vicāra* (pure thoughts), *śuddha-uccāraṇa* (correct pronounciation, which is highly valued in the recitation of sacred texts), and *śuddha-svara* (normal or natural notes in music). Human thoughts, words and musical notes are thus treated (evaluated) as objects are.

Moreover, it is important to note that degrees of *śuddha*-ness are recognized. Gold is thus considered more *śuddha* than, say, copper, so that objects made of gold are always pure—'purified by the movement of air', say the Kashmiri Brahmans—while objects made of other metals require to be purified by washing with water or scrubbing with clay or cowdung and water. Even more significant is the notion that, while certain objects are *śuddha*, others—notably *darbha* grass (*Poa cynosuroides*), gold, food cooked on one's own hearth kept alive by fire originally lit at the time of one's marriage ritual, etc.—are not only pure in themselves but render pure whatever and whosoever comes in contact with them unless he or it is essentially impure (such as human excrement or a Shudra). A Kashmiri Brahman begins certain ritual performances by first putting on the middle finger of his right hand a 'ring' made by twisting together seven blades of *darbha*.[11] This 'ring' is called *pavitra*, that is, something which is itself pure and also purifies the wearer. The most *pavitra* (*paramapavitra*) object for the Brahman is his *yajñopavīta*, the three-stranded cotton neck cord that he wears from the time of his ritual initiation (*upanayana*) onwards and which symbolizes and protects his ritual status as a 'twice-born' (*dvija*) Hindu. At the time of the investiture of the neophyte with the neck cord, the *Gāyatrī mantra*[12] is whispered into his

[11] The seven blades of *darbha* are taken as representing the five senses (*prāṇa*), mind (*mana*) and intellect (*buddhi*). As the *pavitra* is put on the finger, a Sanskrit *mantra* is chanted: 'You [*pavitra*] are a hundred times purifier of the earth; you are a thousand times purifier of gods; you are health-bestowing: I associate you with progeny so that they become rich and abundant in wealth and prosperity.'

[12] Kashmiri Brahmans maintain that the highest knowledge, namely, the true understanding of *Brahman* (*brahma-jñāna*), has been distilled, as it were, in the *Gāyatrī mantra*. It is a prayer to the all-pervading Supreme Deity to bless the devotee with *dhī* or higher intelligence for the attainment of such knowledge. The prayer occurs in the Rig Veda (III.62.10) as also in the Sama and Yajur Vedas.

ear by the family priest and he is thus made *śuddha*, that is, a perfect actor for the performance of rituals and the discharge of the adulthood roles of the householder. Ethnography on the subject of purity and pollution is so detailed, though not always illuminating (see Dumont 1980), that there is little that I can hope to contribute to the discussion beyond what I have written above.

I would, however, like to suggest a relationship between the categories of *śubha* and *śuddha* in relation to the *pātra* or actor.

I take up again the event of childbirth. It is auspicious if it occurs under the right circumstances, defined by the qualities of time, space and the actors concerned, particularly the child and the mother. In actuality, the rightness of circumstances is a matter of degree, for it rarely happens that every factor is without blemish to make the event perfectly auspicious. But even in the best of circumstances, the event renders the child's mother and agnatic kin ritually impure and causes pollution (*aśauca*, a specific expression of *aśuddha*) to them. The child itself is also impure. This pollution, however, pales into insignificance in the light of the joy of the auspicious character of childbirth, particularly the birth of a son, which is duly celebrated through ritual performances and social ceremonies during the following eleven days, culminating in the ritual of purification.

In consonance with such an evaluation of the *śubha* but *aśuddha* aspects of childbirth is the fact that it is not the pollution that death causes which is the matter of deeper concern but the inauspiciousness of the event. My Kashmiri Brahman informants are absolutely unambiguous in their statement of this fact. The pollution wears off (through the passage of time) and is removed (through the performance of rituals) step by step. It is, however, only the occurrence of an auspicious event, most notably the birth of a male child, that finally removes the pall of inauspiciousness which hangs like a dark cloud on a family in which a death has occurred (see Khare 1976a: 185).

Two other types of situation may now be briefly mentioned. First, the situation where both auspiciousness and purity are considered characteristic of an event. Brahmans regard ritual initiation and marriage (the former perhaps more than the latter) as the most notable examples. Second, the situation where inauspiciousness and purity may be found to coexist: but no such situation is acknowledged in practice, emphasizing the overriding quality of auspiciousness.

Speaking specifically about the Kashmiri Brahmans, their attitude to pollution is a pragmatic one. One can avoid contact with many polluting things by the exercise of care or self-restraint. Prescribed procedures, fairly often quite simple (such as washing), are available to remove the consequences of contamination resulting from contact with such things. To be cleansed of pollution when it is unavoidable, one has not only to wash but to do so *immediately*, for example, after evacuation or *after the lapse of a period of time*, as following a birth or death in the family. Mere washing away may not meet the requirement of restoration of ritual status and certain rituals may have to be performed.[13] Moreover, one is pure or impure in relation to someone else or an object or the performance of a particular act in a certain degree. A menstruating woman is severely polluted for the purpose of participation in rituals (particularly the feeding of the manes), but she is not secluded nor required to eat or sleep outside the home.

The daily life of the Kashmiri Brahmans is beset by *śaṅkā*, that is, doubt or perplexity: hesitations as to whether to do something or not, how to do it, when to do it, and so on. The burden of such uncertainty is heavier in the context of the inauspiciousness of certain events than in the context of the impure nature of some things, for the former are not as easily manageable as the latter.[14] A person must watch out, when he

[13] It may be noted here that in *āyurveda*, *śuddhi* refers to the 'purification' of the insides of the body through the administration of enemas and of potions to induce vomitting, blood-letting, etc.; *śuci* refers to purification by ritual means (*mantra*, *japa*, etc.).

[14] Apropos pollution by contact, cf.: 'In this limited sense, impurity is more powerful than purity, but contact here loses something of its religious character: *it does not bring misfortune or disease but only social degradation*' (Dumont and Pocock 1959: 30, emphasis added). I think this is precisely how Kashmiri Brahmans also interpret pollution. It should, however, be noted here that some scholars consider this a norrow interpretation: for instance Das (1977) considers the life/death framework more fundamental and inclusive than the pure/impure or the good-sacred/bad-sacred frameworks. She observes: 'the symbolism of impurity marks off situations which are liminal in the sense that the individual experiences his social world as separated from the cosmic. The paradigm for liminality is provided by death' (ibid.: 120).

sets out from the home on an important errand, lest somebody symbolizing obstruction or failure and, therefore, inauspiciousness be encountered or—if the encounter does take place—allowed to pass by one's right side coming from the opposite direction. Among the most dreaded of such encounters is that with a priest, including one's own family priest, without whose presence no ritual performance, including the auspicious ones, is possible.[15]

Similarly, in Uttar Pradesh, an encounter with a Mahabrahman (who assists at cremations and receives gifts from mourners after a death) is normally considered very inauspicious. However, if he is encountered by a party carrying a dead body for cremation, sighting him is believed to minimize the inauspiciousness of the death and is, therefore, welcome. The unexpected arrival of a sannyasi at a *vidyārambha* (beginning of the study of the sacred texts) ceremony is highly auspicious, but the encounter of a marriage party with him is equally highly inauspicious and, therefore, dreaded. To take a final example, the Brahmans in both Kashmir and Uttar Pradesh consider milk to be one of the purest drinks, to be consumed on auspicious occasions and also offered in worship to deities. It is, however, never consumed at the commencement of a journey, for which occasion yoghourt is the appropriate food, though yoghourt may not be offered to a deity.

The nature of the priest, the Mahabrahman and the renouncer, or of milk and yoghourt, does not change but the significance of different events alters one's relationship to these persons and foods as the normal (not necessarily desirable) life trajectories of the actors involved in them are, as it were, reinforced or deflected and weakened. These examples point to the 'heterogeneousness of time' (Eliade 1974: 147) and the consequent perplexties of the mind in the face of inauspiciousness. The anxiety, fear and emotional disturbance which ominous events give rise to are, according to my informants, much more intense than the doubts regarding correct conduct asso-

[15] See footnote 6 above. Other bad omens recognized by Kashmiri Brahmans include, besides death (particularly during the *pañcaka*), unpleasant dreams, the hooting of owls (symbolizing death and destruction), etc. In Uttar Pradesh the sight of mating crows is considered a portent of many deaths, for crows are identified with ancestors.

ciated with the contact with impure persons, objects and places: my own observation of people's behaviour in rural Kashmir confirms this asservation.

CONCERNING THE CATEGORIES 'ŚUBHA AND 'ŚUDDHA': ETHNOGRAPHIC NOTES AND QUERIES

I now turn to ethnography to explore how the notion of auspiciousness has been handled by anthropologists. I will not undertake a comprehensive survey of literature but confine myself to three authors, namely M. N. Srinivas, R. S. Khare and Frédérique Marglin, each one of whom has devoted considerable attention to this subject, to point out some critical issues that seem to be worthy of clarification and further research. Besides, they provide, between themselves, illustrative material from southern, eastern and northern India.[16]

In his classic study of religion and society among the Coorgs of south India, Srinivas (1952) went into the details of purity and pollution with unprecedented care and also made an important contribution to our understanding of auspiciousness as an aspect of domestic life. It would seem that his earlier study of marriage and the family among various castes of Karnataka, based on his own fieldwork and on published works (see Srinivas 1942), had already sensitized him to this important cultural notion among Hindus. He had thus noted that purchases for a marriage are made and the marriage solemnized on an auspicious day and that married women—the so-called *sumaṅgalī*—are particularly qualified to bless a bride (ibid.: 68–75).

In his second book, Srinivas points out quite early that, according to Coorg belief, 'Every important task must begin in an auspicious moment, or it will fail' (1952: 39). He then dwells on the ritual of *maṅgala* or auspiciousness (ibid.: 70ff), which may be performed on certain happy occasions in the life of an individual but is specifically identified with marriage.

[16] I now find the absence of any discussion of the category of auspiciousness in my account of family and kinship among the Pandits of rural Kashmir (see Madan 1965) rather disconcerting, though not inexplicable. I mentioned auspiciousness and did not confuse it with purity, but did not distinguish between events (weddings) and persons (sons). I also failed to clarify that it was not in sons as such that auspiciousness resides but in what they do—most notably, feeding the manes, begetting sons and continuing the lineage.

Maṅgala is described by him as 'an auspicious or good-sacred ceremony that has to be performed on an auspicious day' (ibid.: 74); the central rite of *mūrta* (derived from the Sanskrit *muhūrta*) in the *maṅgala* complex is performed during a particularly auspicious part of the chosen day. Moreover, the ritual is performed in an 'auspicious' place, such as the ancestral home. *Maṅgala* results in a rearrangement of social structure dramatized by the change in the status of the nubile girl who now becomes a *sumaṅgalī*, that is, one who has a beneficent influence on the lives of other people, obviously by virtue of being herself a blessed person (ibid.: 157).[17] It follows that a widow, who must live alone and not in conjugal bliss,[18] has lost her own blessedness as well as the power to bless.

All this fits in well with the analysis in the previous section of this essay, but it has to be noted that Srinivas does not bring out as clearly as one would have wished the various nuances of meaning in the different uses of the word 'auspicious'. His use of it as a general adjective which defines events, persons and places alike may conceal the fact that in its primary connotation the word refers to an event—to marriage—which produces general well-being (*maṅgala* in Sanskrit). What is perhaps even more regrettable is his decision to include auspiciousness and purity together in the encompassing category of 'good-sacred' without clearly distinguishing between them. He also draws attention to certain formal similarities between actions characteristic of auspicious and inauspicious occasions without providing a discussion of the significance of this formal similarity and of the content of these actions. That 'inversion' occurs is, however, quite obvious.

Commenting on Srinivas's handling of *maṅgala*, Dumont and Pocock (1959: 33) suggest a deeper structure by assimilating auspiciousness into what they consider to be the most funda-

[17] In his account of marriages among Karnataka castes, Srinivas points out that the *tāli*, which the bridegroom ties round the bride's neck, has knots in it made by her mother and other *sumaṅgalī* and is threaded by a prostitute who is referred to as *nitya* (ever)-*sumaṅgalī* (Srinivas 1942: 75). Writing on Tamil women, Reynolds says that *cumaṅkali* literally means an auspicious woman, but clarifies that this auspiciousness does not refer to her own being as a woman but to her relationship with certain significant 'others', notably, her husband and children (1980: 38).

[18] See footnote 4 above (p. 52).

mental of underlying ideas, namely, purity. I do not find this way of resolving the problem of the relationship between auspiciousness and purity quite satisfactory as it ignores the need to examine the independent character of the relations of auspiciousness. The crucial observation in this regard, it may be recalled from the previous section of this essay, is that there are no empirical examples available of the combination of the inauspicious and the pure in a single event, though the other three combinations are exemplified by birth (auspicious-impure), death (inauspicious-impure), and marriage (auspicious-pure)—a fact noted by these authors themselves (though not exactly in the same terms as employed here). Their position is, ultimately, derived from their premise that 'the religion of caste is fundamental' (ibid.: 34).

I now turn to Khare's two books on the cultural significance of food among the Kanyakubja Brahmans of Uttar Pradesh (north India) in which he employs the words 'auspicious' and 'inauspicious' quite extensively. His most general definition of auspiciousness is in terms of those regular happenings which symbolize or seek to bring about a 'pervasive, established domestic value' of collective and comprehensive well-being (1976a: 109, 121n, 185, *et passim*). He clearly sees purity as a value encompassed by the value of auspiciousness. He writes: 'All regular ritual techniques that help establish ritual purity ultimately result in a Hindu householder's constant concern with a morally desirable auspiciousness (for there is no other kind) which, for him, must pervade the ritual and social world if everything between him, his social group and his gods is proceeding properly' (ibid.: 109). Elsewhere, he writes that irrespective of the states of purity and impurity, 'the inauspicious (*aśubha*) should not be allowed to take over in one's household life' (ibid.: 144).

In view of the foregoing, it is surprising that Khare should not have maintained clearly and consistently the distinction between auspiciousness and purity—between events and things—and should have merely written of the 'congruence' between the two (1976b: 71f): the equation that he sets up ('auspiciousness: pure: high:: unauspiciousness: impure: low') breaks down, as—to repeat—birth is an auspicious event but causes pollution. A further blurring of heuristically important distinctions occurs when Khare (like many other scholars) prefixes the adjective 'auspicious' to foods, food areas, cooking utensils, food processing implements, cooking techniques, and even numbers, without bringing out clearly the temporal context. It is, however, only fair to acknowledge that he does draw attention to the character of some objects (such as utensils) as 'definite and dominant symbols of happiness and sorrow' (ibid.: 55) and also points out that certain actions (for example, certain cooking techniques) are similarly symbolic of 'normalcy or auspiciousness or festivity' (ibid.: 62). This is the familiar relation between the signifier and the signified and, one hopes, will be elaborated in future research on the subject.

The third scholar whose work I discuss here is Frédérique Marglin. Her primary concern is with the role of the king and of the *devadāsīs* in the ritual complex associated with the Jagannatha temple at Puri. She pursues her studies along several thematic paths, including notably a richly documented and explicitly articulated discussion of the nature and significance of auspiciousness, purity and power (*śakti*). It is not possible here to undertake a detailed examination of her published and unpublished work (1977, 1985) and I will confine myself to drawing attention to the following aspects of it.

(1) Marglin makes a clear distinction between auspiciousness and purity: the latter is said to pertain to the ordered, hierarchical domain of caste but the former is free flowing. This is best exemplified by the fact that, though the *devadāsīs* are associated with auspiciousness in diverse ways—they dance and sing in the temple every day and on various special occasions; they also sing the joyous songs of well-being (*maṅglagīta*) in the homes of their patrons (the priests of the temple) on happy occasions connected with the life-cycle, most notably marriage—and though they are unfettered by caste regulations, they are yet not allowed to go into the inner sanctum of the temple because they are considered unchaste. Their auspiciousness arises from their being the wives of the god Jagannatha and his representative on earth, the king of Puri; they are *ahya*, ever-married, for the god transcends the mortal domain of birth and death. The *devadāsīs*' impurity results from their being permitted (in fact, expected) to live as concubines of the temple priests who are the servants (*sebākār*) of the

temple god. Their body (*deha*) is, therefore, impure. This essential distinction between auspiciousness/inauspiciousness and purity/impurity (to which I have already drawn attention in the discussion of everyday usages earlier in this chapter) thus seems to be supported by empirical evidence from different domains of life and is also analytically illuminating.

(2) Marglin also presents a list of the cultural meanings, embodiments and 'representatives'—the signifiers—of auspiciousness. It is said to refer to a state of well-being, happiness and pleasure. It is associated with eating and the plentifulness of food; with sexual union, fertility and growth; with progeny and prosperity. It is embodied in, or represented by, water jars, aquatic animals, flags, doors, erotic sculptures, sounds, etc., and, above all, the *devadāsīs*. They are called by Marglin the 'harbingers of auspiciousness'; she also designates them as 'specialists in auspiciousness'.

When Marglin refers to *devadāsīs* as specialists in auspiciousness (and the tribal *daita* as specialists in inauspiciousness), I take it to mean that, though what the *devadāsīs/daitas* do has happy consequences, because their works are ultimately conducive to well-being (*maṅgalakārya*), yet there are elements in the situation in which the *daitas* are involved which are inauspicious, namely, the 'illness' and 'death' of the gods. However, the rejuvenation of the gods also begins at the hands of the *daitas*. The element of the passage of time is important here and, as Marglin illustrates richly, the Hindu conception of it may be more complex than what would be familiar from a Western perspective. Thus, while auspiciousness and the *devadāsīs* are said to symbolize the forward flow of time—the present in relation to the future—inauspiciousness and the *daitas* are related to the reversal of time, that is, death and the past. The *daitas* seem to be of crucial significance as they dramatize the flux of time more sharply than do the *devadāsīs*, so much so that the demarcation between auspiciousness and inauspiciousness itself appears to be arbitrary or is resolved. Marglin does not, however, push her analysis in this direction.

It would be useful to recall here two important distinctions mentioned by me earlier: first, between objects and persons *as such*, on the one hand, and these as symbols, on the other; second, between objects and persons, on the one hand, and events and performances, on the other. When the *devadāsīs* are called *maṅgalanārī* and the songs they sing *maṅgalagīta*, it is clear that two meanings are implied: first, and obviously (even superficially perhaps), these women and their songs contribute to an atmosphere of joy; second, they are associated with happy events whether these occur (births) or are arranged (weddings, pilgrimages). In the process they come to symbolize auspiciousness. Though the distinction between person or act, event and symbol, may be blurred in speech and in the minds of speakers, its validity must not be lost sight of by the analyst.

When pilgrims come to Puri they are told by the priests that seeing and circumambulating *devadāsīs* are auspicious; that is, these actions produce well-being. In the same spirit, worshippers in the temple pick the dust from the feet of dancing *devadāsīs*, or roll on the ground where they have danced, in the hope of attaining well-being, of winning divine grace, for they are told that the *devadāsīs* are the embodiment of Lakshmi.[19] We see here instances of the coalescence of the carrier or bearer of auspiciousness (the *devadāsī*) and its ultimate source (Lakshmi) and this too should be borne in mind.

(3) In her analysis of the consecration ritual within the famous Car Festival (*ratha-yātrā*) ritual complex, Marglin brings out clearly the inter-relatedness of time, place, and person or actor: the *devadāsīs* and the *daitas* are described as doing different things in different parts of the temple on this very special occasion, all contributing to a single though complex task. An actor (*pātra*) in this context stands not merely for a neutral being but an adept, one worthy of receiving the responsibility for a certain role. The issue is that of establishing *pātratā*, that is, one's credentials for the performance of the role. The Brahmans and the *daitas* are born into their role categories; the *devadāsīs* are recruited from different castes for their roles by being dedicated to Jagannatha.

Auspiciousness, then, refers in Marglin's analysis to a situa-

[19] On being told of this, one of my Kanyakubja Brahman informants recalled the myth of the crocodile who tried to drag an elephant into the river to devour him. Thinking its end had come, the elephant, who was a devotee of Vishnu, lifted a lotus with its trunk as a last offering to the god. Vishnu appeared on the scene and redeemed both the elephant and the crocodile: the former for his pure devotion and latter because it had touched the foot of a devotee—itself an act of piety.

tion which enables us to see its constitutive elements in their inter-relatedness and thus in the right perspective. The actor or person (*pātra*), motivated by an explicit purpose (*uddeśya*), and specifically recruited to fulfil it, performs an act or role (*kārya*), in a prescribed manner (*rīti*), in a certain place (*sthāna*), at a specified time (*kāla*), which results in collective well-being (*maṅgala*). That is: the *devadāsī*, dedicated to god, imbued with divine devotion, sings and dances in the outer sanctum of the temple at various times of the day and year: this brings about well-being, just as the feeding of the temple god by the Brahmans does: and the feeding and the dancing take place simultaneously. Dancing, we are further told, symbolizes sexual union in this ritual context. If any one of the elements (purpose, properly accredited actor, the action, the time, and the place) is absent or imperfect, though nothing else is changed, the formal auspiciousness of the situation disappears. To illustrate, the most talented Odissi dancer could not be allowed to dance in the temple for she is not the right *pātra*, although she knows very well how to do it. Similarly, the *devadāsī* may not leave Puri to become a professional dancer and yet retain the right to participate in the ritual complex of the temple, for she would then violate the parameters of time and place and have abandoned the legitimate purpose of her work. Needless to add, what is true of the *devadāsī* is also applicable to the Brahman and the *daita*.

The 'situation', I may add, must be conceptualized in dynamic rather than static terms: it must be seen as an event, a point emphasized earlier in this chapter in the course of my examination of the everyday usage of the words *śubha* and *śuddha*. Time thus appears to be the key element in the situation which illumines the others. In this context the observations of two Uttar Pradeshi Brahman informants—both pundits of the traditional type—appear to be apposite. According to them, *kāla* is the ultimate cause of everything that happens. Its characteristic manifestation is *pravāha* (flow) or *vartana* (movement, circular movement). It is *anādi* (without beginning), *ananta* (without end) and *sarvavyāpaka* (all-pervading, encompassing). Deified as Kala, it is the guardian of life and the upholder of *dharma* (righteousness), and appropriately presides over death. It is not amenable to human control. *Deśa* or *sthāna* (place, location), the informants maintained, is *vyāpya* (permeable, encompassed): it has been created and will be destroyed in time. Human beings realize their being within this framework, in the union of *śakti* and *prakṛti*.[20]

CONCLUDING REMARKS

J. L. Austin once complained that the history of Western philosophy was littered with 'tidy-looking dichotomies', with the student being required to embrace one half or the other (1962: 3). It certainly has not been my intention to propose over-simplifications of this type in respect of the categories *śubha* and *śuddha* in Hindu culture. I have only tried to suggest that certain analytical distinctions are heuristically useful inasmuch as they enable us to understand better the relations and the principles of relationship between the categories under examination.

If auspiciousness/inauspiciousness refers primarily to events —and ultimately to life itself as an event-structure— and if purity/impurity is basically an attribute of objects, why have anthropologists confused the categories by objectifying the events? It would seem that this happened because we have tended to follow too closely what the informants say. Though the informants are usually well aware of behavioural norms and everyday usages, they are not always aware of ambiguities in these. Moreover, they readily—almost unthinkingly—switch from literal to figurative language and back again. In other words, they speak in metaphors, carrying over aspects of events (or objects) to objects (or other objects), and also ignore the distinction between mental and physical concepts, between words and things. Auspicious married women and inauspicious widows are instances of the transferred epithet (see Lakoff and Johnson 1980).

Our task as anthropologists would seem to lie in overcoming ambiguity and decoding figurative language and bringing

[20] Much attention has been devoted to the concepts of *kāla* and *deśa/sthāna* in the Hindu tradition from the Vedas onwards through the *brāhmaṇas*, Upanshads, and Puranas and the two great epics (Mahabharata and Ramayana). The Nyāya-Vaiśeṣika (one of the six systems of Hindu metaphysics) is particularly concerned with these categories (see Bhaduri 1947).

out clearly what we receive through interrogation and observation confusedly. We seek to abstract certain concepts in a cross-cultural framework that hardly concern the people whose culture we study and, therefore, remain inarticulated and unexpressed in it. Auspiciousness is highly meaningful to people in their everyday life but the abstract concept of the passage of time is much less so. Our own hesitation to explicate such concepts perhaps leads us to draw conclusions too soon and at too low a level of generality to produce better understanding.

The present discussion points to the need to explore more systematically than has been done so far the relatively neglected theme of auspiciousness/inauspiciousness in Hindu culture. Of course, this should not be attempted independently of the notion of purity/impurity—for then we would produce only distortions of reality—but in relation to it. The particular expressions and associations of the notion of auspiciousness may vary, but quite clearly it is of basic importance, at least in the scheme of values of upper castes, and is associated with the passage or flux of time and the significance of this fact for human life. If this notion is found closely interlinked with that of purity among upper castes but less so as we move down the ladder, that itself would, far from downgrading the importance of studying it, underscore its potential for deepening our understanding of purity and of the basic elements of Hindu culture.

3

ASCETICISM AND EROTICISM

Should I sojourn in austerity
on the sacred river's bank,
or should I, in worldly fashion,
court women of high grace?

BHARTRIHARI

Free thine self from the threefold nature of things; rise above all opposites, abide always in purity—self-possessed and whole.

BHAGAVAD GITA

INTRODUCTION

In this chapter, based on an essay originally written in honour of Christoph von Fürer-Haimendorf, I follow in his footsteps and make an attempt to examine the problem of moral choices in South Asian societies. I do so in the limited context of the nature–culture dichotomy, which occupies a central place in anthropological literature, and its transformations in Hindu culture.

Fürer-Haimendorf's important study of values and mechanisms of social control in some South Asian societies, *Morals and Merit* (1967), is an invitation to South Asianists generally, and the anthropologists among them particularly, to examine moral concepts in different cultural settings and explore how these enter into the choices that people make. By moral concepts I understand those imperatives of conduct which proclaim what Iris Murdoch (1970) so felicitously calls 'the sovereignty of good', and to which men and women refer when they want to know what is *right* in a certain situation and what one *ought* to do in it—in short, when they are faced with the question, How best to live? Such considerations are especially relevant when people are called upon to make one of those crucial choices which are expected to alter the course of their lives and bestow a new character upon it. Calculations of prudence and utility are here ruled out in principle.

If the central concern of anthropology is with man and woman in relation to culture, then it obviously cannot but be interested in cultural definitions of the problem of human fate and its contingent character. Such an interest entails the study of both the moral choices that people make in a society and the moral concepts or cultural values they invoke in support of their decisions.

Fürer-Haimendorf's approach to the study of moral concepts is comparative in the classical anthropological tradition. He believes that 'there is no society in which the individual is left without guidance and has to make moral choices without reference to social prescriptions' (1967: 224). He also maintains that, 'However divergent the moral systems of two given societies may be, the difference and consequently the mutual incomprehensibility seems to be never as complete as that between two unrelated languages' (ibid.: 11). He sets out, therefore, to look for what he calls the 'common elements' of moral systems, such as 'filial piety, charity, courtesy and truthfulness', which 'can be used in relation to a variety of moral systems' (ibid.: 11–12).

The metaphysical underpinning of the argument in *Morals and Merit* is recognizably and, perhaps, inevitably that of Western philosophy. Within this philosophical tradition there is a well-known argument, going back to Aristotle, according to which man is regarded as being moral by nature, but morality is said to be bestowed not by nature but by culture. In this context, Aristotle's distinction between the intellectual and moral strands of virtue, made in Book II of *Nicomachean Ethics*, may be recalled. According to it, moral virtue is the result of habit, as is obvious from its name *ethike*, which is derived by a slight variation from *ethos*, habit. It follows that specific moral virtues cannot be implanted in us by nature. In Durkheimian terms, this amounts to an affirmation of the categorical imperative of the collective consciousness which guides and constrains individual actors in their pursuits. That such a point of view will greatly appeal to the student of culture, which Fürer-Haimendorf is, need hardly be emphasized here.

There are other traditions that also locate morality—a code—in the actor's nature or substance, but do so in a manner which derives the content of ethical conduct from nature itself: they do not treat the latter as a vessel which may be filled in any way that one likes. The Hindu theory of *guṇa*, as enunciated in the Bhagavad Gita (chapter 14), for instance, is such an alternative viewpoint: put blandly, the moral person is said to be of *sāttvik* or 'good' nature while the evil person is of *tāmasik* or 'dull' nature. Whatever either does is determined by this primal fact.[1] The other viewpoint deriving moral conduct from the pursuit of prescribed actions is also available in the Hindu tradition: while Upanisadic literature stresses innate moral nature, the *dharmaśāstras* emphasize behaviour: in so far as *dharma* is derived from *smṛti*, it is also habit.[2]

The data on which *Morals and Merit* is based are derived from the author's extensive fieldwork among several South Asian societies in central and eastern India and in Nepal, 'ranging from the most primitive of nomadic food-gatherers to the highly civilized adherents of some of the world's great historic religions', namely Buddhism and Hinduism (1967: 207). He almost insists that the anthropologist's data must come from direct observation of conduct and not from a society's 'self-image presented by its own *literati*'. The danger he seems to have in mind is that of a distortion of the ethnographic narrative by subjective bias, but he is quick to acknowledge that 'the anthropological method inevitably involves an element of subjectivity', for the anthropologist has his or her own 'ideological inclinations or unconscious prejudices' (ibid.: 207).

The foregoing acknowledgement of the inevitability of subjectivity in anthropological work encourages me to attempt in this chapter a discussion of moral choices in Hindu culture on the basis of three celebrated works of contemporary Indian fiction. Without at all implying any disagreement with Fürer-Haimendorf's legitimate emphasis on the importance of *observed* conduct, I am concerned here with a discussion of first order interpretations of the kind that the anthropologist's informants are so well known to provide. My informants in the present case happen to be three novelists, and their novels are fragments of

[1] For a well-known discussion of the notion of *guṇa*, see Aurobindo 1950.

[2] I owe this point to Kanti Shah.

the original discourse of contemporary Hindu intellectuals on modes of behaviour characteristic of their society. If a novel appeals to a wide variety of readers, it must tell them something that is of deep concern to them: the art of the narrator-novelist does not by itself explain such wide interest. In fact, Ferdinand de Saussure's dialectical distinction between *langue* and *parole* has been drawn upon by Roland Barthes and others who have suggested that the common cultural background of the author and his public is a condition for the creation of a literary work, that the former is implied by the latter.

Needless to emphasize here, works of fiction are not false though they certainly are a product of creative imagination: they are interpretations fashioned by an artist just as works of ethnography should be interpretations made by the anthropologist. A naive distinction between the 'real' world of the social scientist and the 'imagined' world of the novelist need not detain us here. In fact, it may well be argued that in dealing with human actions and their underlying motives at the most general level, the social scientist has not yet succeeded in going beyond the truly great novelist (see Berger 1978). What is more, in the specific context of the theme of the present essay, it has been suggested that 'What especially the novel does is aid us in the imaginative recreation of moral complexities in the widest sense' (Putnam 1977: 87).

What follows, then, is my attempt to construct a discussion of moral choices in terms of the original discourse provided by the novelist. That my essay itself could be used by a non-Indian student of Indian societies and cultures to construct his own interpretation of Indian culture is another matter and acceptable to me as a legitimate project.

It may be clarified that in the discussion that follows I eschew cross-cultural comparison, not because I consider it unimportant but because the many methodological problems that it raises—above all, that of the comparability of people's own categories of thought—seem very complex to me for adequate treatment in the available space. I therefore concentrate here on what has been called 'thick description'. This is best done by focusing on one culture at a time, and exploring it for the 'structures of inference and implication' (Geertz 1973: 7), of 'signification' (ibid.: 9), which are the object of ethnography.

What one produces thus is an interpretation of patterns of culture in the light of the knowledge that other patterns exist, though not in direct and explicit confrontation with them.

By the very nature of the enterprise, the discussion that follows is not comprehensive but only illustrative. It provides vignettes of moral situations of one type, namely, the clash between asceticism (*tapas*) and eroticism (*kāmuktā*), and seeks to bring out the implications of the choices that people involved in them usually make.

THREE MORAL DISCOURSES

The novels I have chosen for discussion are Bhagvaticharan Varma's Hindi novel *Chitralekha*, U. R. Anantha Murthy's Kannada novel *Samskara*, translated into English by A. K. Ramanujan (the famous Indo-Anglian poet), and Vishnu Sakharam Khandekar's Marathi novel *Yayati*, rendered into Hindi by Moreshvar Tapasvi. Needless to say, my discussion of the three novels is in no way concerned with their literary merit or aesthetic value—I am totally unqualified for such an undertaking, nor is that my intention here. My effort is confined to sorting out the moral choices described and evaluated in them. The presentation of the characters, events and arguments from the novels is selective and interpretive. I have tried not to distort the authors' intentions, though I have throughout paraphrased their language. I have added explanatory comments wherever doing so seemed useful in developing my argument about the nature–culture dichotomy.

Chitralekha was originally published in 1933 and was the work of a young novelist then in his thirties. It has by now acquired the status of a modern classic in Hindi literature. Two Hindi movie versions of it have been made. *Samskara* was published in 1965 and attracted wide attention, particularly after it was made into an award-winning Kannada film in 1970. Anantha Murthy, now in his fifties, teaches English literature at Mysore University. Ramanujan's English translation came out in 1976. *Yayati* was published in 1959 when Khandekar was sixty-one years old and already a renowned littérateur. The novel won him the acclaim of critics and finally, in 1976, a year before his death, the country's prestigious literary award, the Gyanpith Puraskar. It is a long work of almost 180,000 words and more than twice as long as *Chitralekha* or *Samskara*. The Hindi translation by Tapasvi was published in 1977.

Situational morality: a snare?

Chitralekha opens with a question which two disciples ask of their guru: they would like to know what *pāpa* is, it being presumed that they have already been instructed in the nature and significance of its binary opposite, *puṇya*. It is very difficult to translate these terms, but I will follow the general practice and render *pāpa* as 'immoral' or 'wicked' and *puṇya* as 'moral' or 'meritorious' (Monier-Williams 1976).

The guru says that he does not know what *pāpa* is, having no personal experience of it, suggesting that deductive reasoning will fail to provide an answer. He therefore decides to send the two young men to discover for themselves what *pāpa* is. One of them, a Brahman, is sent to become a disciple of a great yogi, Kumaragiri, and the other, a Kshatriya, is assigned as a servant to a feudal aristocrat, Bijagupta. The scene is laid in the capital city of Pataliputra and its environs during the days of the king Chandragupta Maurya (*c.* 310 B.C.). Kumaragiri and Bijagupta emerge as the two protagonists in the story and represent not merely two life-styles but, in fact, two apparently opposed moral choices.

Kumaragiri, as already stated, is a yogi. Though youthful, he claims to have overcome all bodily desires and worldly attachments and found what he considers true happiness. Worldly life is to him the means to an end which is the life beyond corporeal existence. He is a scholar and an adept in ritualistic practices and has spiritual attainments to his credit. The peculiar combination of youth and non-attachment has given him the unique distinction of possessing both an effulgent presence and moral power. Kumaragiri represents the principle of culture or refinement (*saṁskṛti*) as against that of untamed nature (*prakṛti*), of the spirit (*ātmā*) as against the material body (*śarīra*); he embodies in himself a moral choice which proclaims the superiority of asceticism over eroticism.

Bijagupta is the opposite type: he is a young, handsome and wealthy feudal lord of high social status. Worldly attachments and joys, here and now, are the *summum bonum* of his life. Though unmarried, he has an apt companion in Chitralekha, the city's most gifted and celebrated dancer. She is an intelligent and cultured person, and shares with Bijagupta his world-view. Born a Brahman, widowed at an early age, involved subsequently in a love affair, mother of an illegitimate child, life's ironies have led her through several changes of fortune into the affection of Bijagupta. Though his mistress, she lives independently of him, in a style which matches his. Together, they aver the value of natural bodily appetites and their satisfaction as the supreme source of happiness. They consider the self-control and self-denial of the ascetic destructive not only of the human body but of the soul itself. In their own eyes, and in the eyes of many people, their life too represents a moral choice which proclaims the superiority of life-affirming eroticism (using the word in its broadest sense) over life-denying asceticism, of the *bhogī* over the yogi.[3]

The sequence of events which brings out the implications and significance of these choices is triggered off by a chance encounter between Kumaragiri and Bijagupta and Chitralekha when the latter two seek shelter in his hermitage one night. Kumaragiri is greatly upset by the presence of a woman in his hut. On Bijagupta's inquiry as to why an ascetic, who has acquired mastery over his senses, should be reluctant to give shelter to a woman, Kumaragiri answers that woman represents the darkness of attachment, desire and illusion and has no place in the world of knowledge. This leads to a discussion between him and Chitralekha over such metaphysical issues as appearance or the relativity of perception and reality or the-thing-in-itself. The encounter produces an unusual result: the yogi sees knowledge as the dancer's most outstanding attribute and she finds him an irresistibly handsome man.

This encounter is followed by another in the royal court where Kautilya, the king's chief adviser, is expounding on the

[3] To introduce a cross-cultural reference from the Japanese literary tradition, the myth portions of *Kojiki* and *Nihongi* would seem to support a similar view: 'Morality lies in the total sympathy of one person for another, in the desire to give, not humanitarian "rights", but human fulfilment, even as he receives the same common and essential gift. In a real sense, morality derives from the forms of love' (Pelzel 1974: 23).

conflict between statecraft and justice (*nīti*) on the one hand, and religious and moral duty (*dharma*) on the other. Kautilya is a rationalist and a pragmatist and considers morality, religion and even God as cultural constructs and, therefore, subject to criticism and rational reformulation. Kumaragiri, also present in the court, is unable to match Kautilya's logic but demonstrates spiritual power by performing a miracle.[4]

Chitralekha, who is also the court dancer, engages the yogi in argument and succeeds in making him confess that he had resorted to the performance of a miracle because he could not establish by argument the existence of a divine being or the supremacy of *dharma*. Defending himself, he emphasizes the importance of faith and imagination for the seeker of the spirit. Chitralekha is, however, judged by the court to have won the argument. Kumaragiri also knows this to be true; his particular sense of defeat arises from the fact that he has been vanquished in a philosophical debate by a 'fallen' woman, a mere dancer.

Defeated and dismayed, Kumaragiri retires to his hermitage but is visited there by Chitralekha. She tells him that she has come to receive spiritual instruction from him; but actually she is in love with him. The yogi finds the situation incomprehensible: how can one devoted to the body's pleasures possibly become a seeker of things spiritual? Chitralekha tries to silence his doubts, saying she has turned her back on her past. She knows, however, that she poses a threat to his whole being. This is, in fact, the threat that the realm of nature seemingly always poses to that of culture. While the human agent seeks *puṇya*, he is pursued by *pāpa*.

Moreover, Chitralekha tries to teach Kumaragiri a view of the nature of woman contrary to that enunciated by him at their first meeting. Woman is spiritual power (*śakti*), she says, and the principle of creation. He who fears woman is unworthy of his humanity. Kumaragiri begins to experience, besides the power of her intellect, the attraction of her bodily beauty. He holds his ground, nevertheless, refusing to accept her as a disciple. He tells her that if he consents to impart spiritual instruction to her, he fears he will himself end by becoming her

[4] I am not sure whether the novelist's interpretation of Kautilya's view would be accepted by the scholars concerned with exegeses of the *Arthashastra*. This is not, however, important from my point of view.

devotee, and that he is not prepared for such a reversal of roles. The vulnerability of his own moral choice is apparent to him.

Chitralekha decides to leave Bijagupta. She informs him that she thinks she has become a burden on him and, therefore, ought to pull out of his life so that he can marry. However, she pledges eternal love for Bijagupta, love based on the union of souls rather than that of bodies. She thus recommends the transformation of the carnal relationship into a spiritual one.

Seeing through Chitralekha's protestations, Bijagupta is greatly shaken by the turn of events. Without seeking it, he is thrown into the company of another feudal lord and his daughter, Yashodhara, while on a visit to Kashi. Yashodhara had earlier been offered to him in marriage but he had refused the offer, saying that, though he was formally unmarried, he considered Chitralekha his wife. For him this was a question of moral judgement rather than legal fact: marriage is not an event, he had said, but an everlasting physical-cum-spiritual bond between man and woman.

On one occasion an interesting conversation takes place between Bijagupta and Yashodhara about nature (*prakṛti*) and culture (*saṁskṛti*), which is directly relevant to the present essay. He is unmoved by her unbounded enthusiasm for nature and its beauty, and draws her attention to its harsh and ugly aspects. He also points out to her that, from the point of view of human beings, nature is incomplete. Human creations, without which life is impossible, have their origin in nature's imperfections.

Bijagupta subsequently has an encounter with a sannyasi who tells him that, though the creations of culture are intended to lighten the burden of nature, they are artificial and must not be regarded as being constitutive of life: such an attitude amounts to a denial of life itself. Culture extends and refines nature but, in the process, sets up its own tyranny. On another occasion, Bijagupta expounds a monistic doctrine in a discussion with Yashodhara's father, describing renunciation as not the opposite of attachment but only a change of the 'locus' of love. These conversations bring out the untenability of conventional oppositions and point to the need for a transcendental view of nature and culture, of asceticism and eroticism, according to which the whole is a dialectical synthesis of apparently antithetical elements.

Meanwhile, Chitralekha has gone to Kumaragiri's hermitage. They undergo a transformation: she becomes genuinely interested in spiritual life and he falls in love with her: the erotic urge becomes the ascetic quest and *vice versa.* It is now Kumaragiri who propounds the doctrine of attachment and love of an embodied being. He who calls himself the renouncer or the unattached man (*virāgī*) is, in fact, attached to the divine (*brahma*). The love of the divine must include the love of all beings. He tells Chitralekha that for him she is now the goal of his life. She, in turn, extols the virtue of self-control and advises him to try to conquer himself and not her—to try to seek the spirit and not the body. Finally, overwhelmed by desire, Kumaragiri lies to Chitralekha that Bijagupta has married Yashodhara. This is a blow Chitralekha finds hard to bear and, in her shock, she gives herself up to Kumaragiri.

Bijagupta is faced with his own moral choice. Considering himself free of any obligation to Chitralekha, who has left him of her own accord, he finds himself drawing emotionally closer to Yashodhara and contemplates marriage with her. He, however, learns from Shvetanka, his companion—the same person who has come to him to find out what *pāpa* is—that the latter is in love with Yashodhara. His first reaction is to ask Shevatanka to move out of his way, but then he changes his mind: he makes his choice guided by the value of self-sacrifice. He advises Yashodhara's father to marry her to Shvetanka. To make this possible, he transfers all his wealth and property to Shvetanka: in the process, he bestows the social rank of a feudal lord on the young man. Bijagupta thus becomes a renouncer himself. On learning of all this, and of Kumaragiri's deception to her, Chitralekha gives up Kumaragiri and her wealth, and joins Bijagupta in the quest of the spirit.

A year has passed since the guru sent out his two disciples to discover through their experience the significance of *pāpa.* They now return to him, each affirming the virtues of his own master. The guru points out to them that human beings are not autonomous moral agents at all; they are not free but engulfed in situations in the making of which they play no part. People neither commit sins nor perform meritorious acts:

they simply do what they have to do, they make the choice dictated by their situation (*paristhiti*). The notion of 'situation' obviously includes the actor's own self as moulded by his or her previous choices. To that extent, I would suggest, one's situation includes the element of freedom.[5]

The moral discourse in *Chitralekha*, it seems to me, denies the validity of the notion of untrammelled free will, though not of moral choices as such. It clearly emphasizes the virtue of the concern of a moral agent for the well-being of others. (In this respect, the novelist goes against the logic of his own argument when, in the end, he equates Bijagupta and Kumaragiri in the moral balance.) The novel questions a simplistic notion of moral choices which opposes wickedness to merit, body to soul, and eroticism to asceticism. In *Samskara*, too, the focus is on the problematic moral agent. but the treatment of the question takes place along a different line of argument.

Authenticity as morality

The scene in *Samskara* is a Karnataka hamlet called Durvasapura; the time is, perhaps, the 1930s or '40s. It could have been any other time, any other century: Ramanujan, the translator, vividly calls it (in his Afterword) Indian Village Time. Legend links the village to the mythological figure Durvasa. It is well known because of this and because it is the home of two unusual Brahmans, Praneshacharya and Naranappa, the protagonists in the narrative.

Praneshacharya had, even when only a boy, unusual ideals: he wanted to be free of all passions. At the age of sixteen he chose to marry a twelve-year old girl born an invalid. He hoped thus to earn merit through austerity and self-sacrifice. He studied scriptures and went to Kashi where he earned encomiums. Since then his life has been spent in the performance of rituals, in study, in giving instruction to others, and in serving his invalid wife—all this in the spirit of duty, without concern for immediate reward. He hoards 'his penances like a

[5] Cf. the Upanishadic position as stated by Hiriyana (1949: 47): 'Freedom should be regarded as consisting not in unrestricted licence, but in being determined by oneself.' This is the same injunction as Matthew Arnold's call to be 'self-govern'd, at the feet of Law'.

miser his money',[6] hoping ultimately to 'get ripe and ready' for the highest spiritual attainments. He has so completely overcome bodily appetites that, though his public readings of erotic tales from Sanskrit literature sometimes drive young men into sexual frenzy, he himself is totally unaffected by them. He is truly an ascetic. His fellow Brahman villagers, even those older than him, respect and honour him. His word is to them as authoritative as sacred scripture. He alone among them is the *ācārya*, teacher. The story opens with an occasion on which his advice is, indeed, very much needed.

Naranappa, who represents in the novel the erotic-epicurean human type, has died of plague and the Brahmans must decide how to cremate the corpse. Though born a Brahman, he had done everything a Brahman should not do. He had deserted his wife and taken a beautiful low-caste woman, Chandri, daughter of a prostitute, as his mistress. He not only lived with her in the hamlet but also ate food cooked by her, and had thus lost his ritual purity. He consumed meat and drank liquor. He ridiculed the rituals of fellow-Brahmans, threw into the river the holy idol that his kinsfolk had worshipped for generations, and dynamited the fish in the sacred temple pond. He 'corrupted' Brahman youth, enticing them into drama, dance and music. Naranappa had Muslim friends whom he brought into his house, and subsequently dared the Brahmans to excommunicate him so that he might become a Muslim. He repeatedly challenged Praneshacharya: 'Let's see who wins in the end—you or me.' And Praneshacharya had always hoped to win Naranappa back to good brahmanical ways and thus earn merit for himself.

While alive, Naranappa was an enemy of the Brahmans of Durvasapura. Now dead, he is a nuisance: till his body is cremated no adult in the hamlet may eat. He had never ceased to be a Brahman though he had not lived as one. Would it be all right for his kinsmen to cremate him? If not, who should

[6] Whereas I have avoided direct quotation from *Chitralekha* and *Yayati*, I have done otherwise in the case of *Samskara*. The reason for this is not merely the fact that the language of this essay and Ramanujan's translation of the novel are the same; more importantly it is the fact that the most crucial portion of *Samskara* is a presentation not of events or characters but of Praneshacharya's dialogue with himself, and it seemed best to preserve its flavour as captured by a gifted translator who is equally at home in both Kannada and English.

do so? No non-Brahman could be allowed to touch a Brahman's dead body. This is the problem to which Pranesacharya is asked to find a solution. His task is complicated by the fact that if he decides to entrust the cremation to Naranappa's kinsmen, he must decide which of them is to do so: with the responsibility for cremation would go the right to the gold ornaments which Chandri, who received them from Naranappa, has offered to defray the funeral expenses. Praneshacharya retires to consult the texts for an answer but fails to find it by nightfall.

Not only have the Brahmans waited for Praneshacharya's verdict; Chandri, too, has patiently done so. Unable to withstand hunger, she goes into a banana grove, eats some fruit and drinks from the flowing stream. She is, in fact, part of the same bountiful nature to which the bananas and the flowing waters belong. She has lived all her life outside the laws of Brahmans: she has been an exception to all rules, ever-auspicious, daily-wedded, without widowhood and, in a sense, without sin or blame like the flowing river in which people wash their impurities and out of which they emerge purified.

Chandri awaits Praneshacharya's decision and thinks about his gentleness and kindness. She wonders whether this great teacher and ascetic has ever known anything about the body's pleasures. As yet childless, she recalls that her mother used to say that prostitutes should get pregnant by holy men such as Praneshacharya, who Chandri knows is virtuous and handsome. But it was not easy to be so blessed by such a man. She is woken from her reveries by the *ācārya* himself who comes out to return to her the gold ornaments: her generosity had only complicated matters. He gently reminds her that, though Naranappa is dead, she has her life to live and provide for.

The next day Praneshacharya decides to seek divine guidance in the Maruti temple. The Brahmans and Chandri wait, but there is no answer from the god, and the night falls a second time on the hamlet and on Naranappa's rotting body. Chandri has visited the banana grove again, to eat, but is now back outside the temple. Praneshacharya remembers his crippled wife and leaves the temple to minister to her needs. Chandri follows him in the forest, full of compassion and gratitude to him, distressed that he should suffer for her sake. She wants to touch his feet in reverence but ends up clutching his legs against her bosom. Praneshacharya, bewildered but full of pity for her, strokes her hair, but words fail him and he cannot utter the blessing. She rises to press him to herself.

'Touching full breasts he had never touched, Praneshacharya felt faint. As in a dream, he pressed them. The strength in his legs ebbing, Chandri sat the *ācārya* down, holding him close. The *ācārya*'s hunger, so far unconscious, suddenly raged, and he cried out like a child in distress, "O Amma!" Chandri leaned him against her breasts, took the plantains out of her lap, peeled them and fed them to him. Then she took off her sari, spread it on the ground, and lay on it hugging Praneshacharya close to her, weeping, flowing in helpless tears.'

They wake up from the experience with opposite feelings about it. Chandri hopes that she may have become pregnant and thus earned merit: 'a natural in pleasure, unaccustomed to self-reproach', she feels 'a sense of worthwhileness, like the fragrance of flowers hidden'. As for Praneshacharya, he knows he is lost. All the rules of culture that he had so assiduously learnt lie in ruins, and nature, manifested through hunger for food and sexual desire, triumphs. The sad fragility of the ascetic choice is revealed. He had always believed that no one chooses to be good, that some people—such as himself—are born with the good nature that leads them to make the right choices. This belief in inborn *guṇa*, too, is taken away from him.

Chandri goes home to the decomposing corpse. Unable to bear the situation any longer, she asks one of Naranappa's Muslim servants to cremate the body, which he does during the night without anybody else's knowledge. Chandri then leaves the village having fulfilled her roles, as it were, in the play.

Praneshacharya also goes back to his home and his dependent wife and to the anxious Brahmans. He is filled with remorse but also experiences 'a lightness in the thought' that he is now 'a free man, relieved by the prostitute of his responsibility to lead the way, relieved of all authority', of the burden of being the guru and the *ācārya*. A Sanskrit chant which he had learnt by heart and recited daily, rises in his mind: 'I am sin, my work is sin, my soul is sin, my birth is in sin.' But he then thinks: 'No, no, even that is a lie. Must forget all words learned by heart, the heart must flow free like a child's.' This represents a return to spontaneity, to nature, and a resolve to break with memory, with culture: it is a bid for escape from the tyranny of culture. 'Even if he had left desire, desire had not left him.'[7]

The lives of Praneshacharya and Naranappa are strangely but significantly a mirror image of each other. Naranappa, too, had left his brahmanical culture, but brahmanical culture had not left him. The body in relation to culture is, the novelist implies, the source of the problem in both cases, the body pulsating with desire no less than the body rotting away; the one polluted and the other polluting.

Praneshacharya's ties with the Brahman community are already snapped in his own eyes. He tells them, 'I'm lost. I couldn't get Maruti to say anything. I know nothing. You do whatever your hearts say.' The Brahmans decide to seek the advice of another *ācārya* elsewhere, and leave Praneshacharya to his memories and reflections.

'So far he didn't even live; doing only what was done, chanting the same old mantra, he had remained inexperienced. Experience is risk, assault. A thing not done before, a joining in the dark of the jungle. . . . Just as he had received the touch of woman, did Naranappa receive the touch of God in the dark, unbidden?' (This is comparable to the notion of 'cloistered virtue' in the Western tradition.) Had not Naranappa once taunted him that, if only Brahmans would be like the sages of their holy legends and eat food cooked by low-caste women and make love to them, they would experience God? Dualities must, then, be meaningless and all choices expressions of moral arrogance.

Praneshacharya remembers his childhood fascination for alternately swimming in the river and drying himself on the hot sand. The long repressed body comes alive and his senses reawaken. He rushes to the spot where he and Chandri had united and smells the grass on which they had lain and made love. This is a most remarkable passage in the novel, in which an entire orchestra of senses are shown awakened in unison,

[7] Ron Inden and Kanti Shah have drawn my attention to comparable notions in nineteenth-century European romanticism.

rising to a crescendo. But the hold of culture is only loosened, not cast off: the *ācārya* again remembers his wife. He goes home to find her dead: plague has claimed her too, totally impartial between a sinner and a saint's blameless wife. Without more ado, he takes her body away for cremation.

He does not return home, leaves everything behind and sets off from Durvasapura, going wherever his feet might take him, thinking he is now free, without duties or debts. He does not even want to remember God, just stand alone. But can one do so? 'Whatever his decision, his feet still walked him close to the habitations of men. This is the limit of his world, his freedom.' Being free and alone is also self-deception, just as being chained to cultural rules and fellow human beings is. Is one totally helpless, then, at the mercy of circumstances? His 'moment' with Chandri had just happened, by God's will, as it were.

'Even if I lost control, the responsibility to decide was still mine. Man's decision is valid because it is possible to lose control, not because it is easy. We shape ourselves through our choices, bring form and line to this thing we call our person. Naranappa became the person he chose to be. I chose to be something else and lived by it. But suddenly I turned at some turning. I'm to answer for it. What happened at that turning? Dualities, conflict, rushed into my life. . . . How did the ancient sages face such experiences? Without dualities, conflict? One wonders . . .'. One can, perhaps, remake oneself 'in full wakefulness', but what moral authority does one have to include another's life in one's decision? 'O God, take from me the burden of decision' is Praneshacharya's anguished prayer, uttered in total loneliness.[8]

Praneshacharya, at the end of the story, waits, 'anxious, expectant'. *Samskara* ends on this note—the characteristic existentialist possibility or impasse. As Ramanujan puts it (in his Afterword), 'the novel ends, but does not conclude'.

[8] I have omitted mention of various incidents involving Praneshacharya during the day after his departure from Durvasapura; his thought process, as described in the novel, seemed more important to me for the purpose of this essay. It may be stated here, however, that these incidents sharpen Praneshacharya's consciousness of the oppressiveness of culture, of alienation, on the one hand, and of the impossibility of a retreat into himself, withdrawn from society, on the other.

Anantha Murthy suggests authenticity, rather than an opposition between body and spirit, between eroticism and asceticism, as the ultimate criterion of moral choices. He does not share Bhagvaticharan Varma's passive attitude towards situations. He also implies the virtue of transcendence as the way out of dualities, though he considers its realization highly problematic. Vishnu Sakharam Khandekar, however, asserts it confidently and at length in *Yayati.*

Transcending moral choice-making through detachment

Yayati is based on an episode in the great epic poem Mahabharata which is also found in the Bhagavata and several other puranic texts. The locale is Hastinapur and the time mythological. Yayati is a king's son. When still a young boy, his mother had made him promise that he would never abandon his home. The reason for this rather curious request was that her elder son, Yati (*yati* actually means 'ascetic' or renouncer) had already done so. He had learnt of the curse, pronounced on his father by a sage whom he had insulted, to the effect that his children would never be happy. The prospect of an unhappy life had led Yati to decide to become a sannyasi, though he was then only a teenager. This had happened before Yayati's birth. Yayati had promised his mother that he would become a victorious warrior, never a renouncer. The boy had a romantic streak in him and might well have become a poet, but he strove hard to fulfil his royal destiny and his martial choice. The instruction he received from his elders on the importance of temporal power and the worthwhileness of worldly life helped him in his endeavour.

Yayati, now a brave and talented young man, well versed in everything a prince ought to know, persuades his father to perform *aśvamedha,* the horse sacrifice of 'world' conquest and victory. He follows the horse all over the country to protect it against capture. In the course of these wanderings he has an encounter in a forest with a recluse engaged in the mortification of his body. The recluse talks to Yayati about the unworthiness of princes for they are usually given to soul-killing sensual pleasures. This yogi turns out to be Yati.

Yayati asks Yati what his quest is, why he is subjecting himself to the ordeal of *haṭhayoga,* eating only bitter fruit and roots and sleeping on thorns. Yati answers that the body is a human being's worst enemy, for he who devotes himself to the body's rapture never experiences spiritual joy. To vanquish the body and win control over one's senses is, however, far more difficult than killing one's enemies and winning royal victories. The implications of the ascetic as against the royal choices are thus apparent.

Yayati's next encounter is with a gifted young man like himself, Kach, son of the great sage Brihaspati, guru of the gods. Kach teaches Yayati a different doctrine from that of Yati. The body's rapture is natural and no immorality attaches to it so long as the body is held subordinate to the spirit. Nature is not to be denied: it should be reshaped by culture. The goals of life (*puruṣārtha*), Kach says, do not exclude rational worldly pursuits (*artha*), nor aesthetic and sensual pleasures (*kāma*) either, but these must be subsumed under righteous conduct (*dharma*). Encompassed in moral conduct, worldly pursuits are worthwhile and, indeed, moral. The *dharma* of the king, or of the ordinary householder is in no way morally inferior to renunciation. The ultimate human quest, whatever one's station in life, however, should be to rise above the body and sensual pleasures and strive for spiritual fulfilment and joy (*ānanda*).

But Yayati is a prince and he soon learns to appreciate bodily pleasures. Wine and the experience of carnal love fill his life. And then, on his father's death, he becomes the king of Hastinapur. Meanwhile, Kach has become a pupil of the great sage Shukracharya, guru of the daemons. He has many virtues: knowledge, wisdom, confidence, humility, gentleness of disposition, and, above all, concern for others combined with non-attachment.

Shukracharya's daughter, Devayani, falls in love with Kach. Though he is also attracted to her, he avoids her, for his quest is of the spirit. He also wins the affection and respect of Sharmishtha, daughter of the king of daemons. He tells her of his quest. He confesses to her his love for Devayani but adds that true ennobling love must make one look beyond one's own self. The fulfilment of moral obligation is the highest virtue. Love is thus not to be opposed to duty but absorbed into it.

Subsequently, Devayani meets Yayati by chance and asks

him to marry her, which he does after some initial hesitance. Sharmishtha, who has been a friend of Devayani, is obliged to become the latter's maid in punishment for an impulsive act of defiance. The conjugal life of the royal couple has a troubled beginning because of differences in the life-styles of the Brahman wife and the Kshatriya husband. Yayati, nevertheless, finds much happiness in his physical relationship with Devayani, so much so that he cannot bear to think of giving it up. His quest for understanding and love, however, remains unfulfilled. The union of Yayati and Devayani is a meeting of two bodies but not of two souls.

Finding the occasion for a ritual performance, Devayani invites Kach, whom she has never quite ceased to love nor forgiven for refusing to marry her, to her husband's court. He arrives with Yati, who behaves in a manner which others find difficult to understand and they judge him to be mad. For instance, he wants Sharmishtha to be given to him so that he transform her into a 'man'. Later, some people claim they saw him walk across the flooded river at night and leave the city. Obviously, Yati has acquired the superhuman powers of a *haṭhayogi* but has failed to come to terms with human nature. Woman's very being appears a great threat to him.

Kach provides an explanation for Yati's strange behaviour. Yati's view of life is unfortunately flawed inasmuch as it is mono-dimensional. His early decision to try to find God has resulted in the death of the human being in him. Human life is based on pairs of opposites or *dvandva* (which could be mutually reinforcing or destructive), and he who denies this fundamental principle is bound to come to grief. It is true that the sannyasi finds spiritual joy only when he succeeds in transcending dualities; even so, one must begin with the recognition that both the terms of a duality are equally important. The problem is not to separate them but to establish a proper relationship between them at a higher, transcendent level. The soul, after all, resides in the body and not independently of it. Yati's mistake is that he denies part of his own being, that which belongs to the domain of nature.

Man acquires merit not by denying the existence of the body and its appetites, but by refining them and bringing them under the control of his will (*saṁyama*). The mature or cultured person is one who has distanced himself from nature but not broken away from it. Reason must always command the senses: it must encompass them. One who posits a sharp dichotomy between body and soul has a distorted view of life. Man is the very best, the finest, link between nature and culture. Dualities are not an attribute of the domain of nature, and god (*brahma*) and the domain of the spirit are beyond them. It follows that dualities are an attribute of human intelligence and, therefore, the basis for moral judgement. The only viable view of human life is one based on a balanced and harmonized relationship (*santulan*) between the body, the mind and the soul.

Kach's logic is lost on Yayati and Devayani. Their temperaments continue to be wide apart, though they live together. Yayati finds understanding from Sharmishtha and mutual love develops between them. They marry secretly—doing so being permissible (*gandharva vivāha*)—and Devayani knows nothing about their relationship. Both women give birth to sons. Devayani has her suspicions about Yayati's relationship with the other woman, and he senses this. Fearing that Devayani might have Sharmishtha and her son murdered, Yayati arranges to have them sent away from the city. There is complete estrangement between him and Devayani, who succeeds in finding out the truth about the relationship between the two lovers. She therefore forbids Yayati to touch her body. The bodies separated, their relationship loses its sole basis and is reduced to a mere arrangement.

For the next eighteen years Yayati makes bodily pleasures the constitutive principle of his life. He lives by a simple hedonistic doctrine: there is no merit or sin in human life, only pleasure (*sukha*) or pain (*dukha*). He pursues pleasure but never finds happiness. *Mṛgayā* (hunting), *madirā* (wine) and, above all, *madirākṣī* (woman) become his principal preoccupations. The more he indulges in dissipation, the more insatiable his desires become.

Yayati now becomes Yati's opposite and, like him, a deranged person, losing all sense of the supreme value of balance in human life and therefore unable to judge his own moral condition. 'Am I in heaven—or am I in hell?' is the question he asks himself. Reflecting on his condition he comes to formulate the distinction between worldly happiness and spiritual joy. He realizes that his mistake has been the unbridled pursuit of pleasure. He contrasts his life with that of Kach who, too, had been attracted to Devayani. But Kach had placed his moral obligation towards others above his personal happiness.

Yayati's life is completely reshaped at this stage by a curse. Devayani's father, Shukracharya, emerges from meditation to find what Yayati has done to himself and his wife. He asks for an explanation and Yayati tells him that his has been the foolishness of youth, whereupon the sage curses him and Yayati suddenly becomes a very old man. The desires and hopes of a younger man, however, remain alive in his wizened frame. Shukracharya is, happily, persuaded to relent and he promises that Yayati can get back his youth if someone related to him by blood will exchange his own youthful body for the king's aged one.

Shukracharya's coming to Hastinapur has coincided with the return of Devayani's son, the prince Yadu, from a battle in which he was taken prisoner but later released when the enemy was defeated by Sharmishtha's son, Puru. Puru, who lives outside Hastinapur, is aware of his parentage and blood ties with Yadu, and has rushed to obtain his release from his enemies. Yadu brings Puru to the court without knowing who he is. Yayati asks Yadu if he will exchange his body with his own and succeed him immediately as king. Yadu refuses this favour, but Puru offers his body, declaring that he is Yayati's and Sharmishtha's son. The wish having been expressed and accepted, Yayati becomes young again and Puru is instantly transformed into an old man.

Remorse now seizes Yayati. Kach's yogic powers, however, help to restore the original bodily condition of Puru. Kach reminds Yayati that culture, which has no place in the life of animals and seems so important in life, in fact alters man only superficially. Man must therefore be ever vigilant to maintain the control of his will over the senses and realize the futility of a life ordered to an exclusive fulfilment of human desires.[9] It is

[9] The story of Yayati in the traditional texts has many ramifications (see, for example, O'Flaherty 1976: 237–43), with which I am not concerned here. Thus, according to a widely read popular presentation of the Mahabharata, Yayati does not suffer from any feeling of immediate remorse but spends many more years

thus suggested by Vishnu Khandekar that the only true moral basis of worldly life can be self-sacrifice, which is what detachment (*virakti*) is really all about, and not self-seeking. It is through detachment rather than formal renunciation that all dualities are transcended.

CONCLUDING OBSERVATIONS

In the foregoing presentation of three moral discourses, I have made an attempt to present some related conceptualizations of an Indian view of moral choices. These formulations proceed characteristically and contrary to the Western sociological tradition, from personal-soteriological towards social-ethical concerns, rather than the other way round. According to this view, though criteria for such choices are available (for instance, self-sacrifice for the good of others), the ideal that human beings should ultimately strive for is the attainment of a level of self-consciousness (*ātma-jñāna*) which transcends the need for moral choices of the either/or kind. This is *mokṣa*, release from volition. Max Weber, Albert Schweitzer and many other Western scholars have dismissed this as moral quietism, but it does not appear as such to Hindus.

Such a view of moral choices can be traced back to Upanishadic philosophy (see Radhakrishnan 1953: 15–145 *et passim*) and is also stated in the Bhagavad Gita, the most widely read Hindu scripture.[10] I am, of course, not suggesting that the novels on which this essay is based are formal expositions of

---

engrossed in worldly enjoyments. Later he goes to the splendorous garden of Kubera, the lord of wealth, and lives there in the company of a celestial courtesan. Finally, 'wisdom' dawns on him and he returns to his son and tells him: 'Dear son, sensual desire is never quenched by indulgence any more than fire is by pouring ghee in it. I had heard and read this, but till now I had not realized it. No object of desire—corn, gold, cattle or women—nothing can ever satisfy the desire of man. We can reach peace only by a mental poise beyond likes and dislikes. Such is the state of Brahman. Take back your youth and rule the kingdom wisely and well' (Rajagopalachari 1968: 38).

[10] Cf.: 'The dualism between body and spirit is not radical. Without maltreating the body we can attain the freedom of the spirit . . .' (Radhakrishnan 1940: 98). Again: 'We are not called upon to crush the natural impulses of human life. . . . The aim of ascetic discipline is the sanctification of the entire personality' (ibid.: 99).

transcendentalism, or accurate ones, but only indicating that a major source of influence in the fragmented consciousness of contemporary Hindu intellectuals continues to be an ancient one. It is an influence which one also detects in Sanskrit poetry and drama, in which the moral life reflects the merger of earthly and heavenly loves (Hindery 1978: 157–76 *et passim*).

The scope of this essay is, however, deliberately confined to the consideration of moral choices in some contemporary literary texts and in the specific context of the nature–culture dichotomy as manifested in the choice of an erotic or an ascetic mode of life. It is important to note here that in either case it is his or her whole being which should be the actor's main concern. The human body is a key symbol which bridges nature and culture but does not by itself constitute the totality of being. Any effort to locate the body exclusively in either of these two domains is a bad choice, for it is bound to fail. But this bridge is no simple architectural concept. The close but complex relationship between eroticism and asceticism has long been recognized in Indian thought: it has characteristically found rich expression in Hindu mythology, particularly in the Shiva and Krishna myths.[11]

All three discourses, then, question a simplistic dualistic conception of the moral domain and, therefore, of the viability of choices which are based on a simple-minded opposition of *pāpa* and *puṇya*. It is shown that those who seek the latter are dogged by the former, and those who seem morally derelict turn out to be worthy of being the recipients of divine grace. Each novel opens with a categorization of characters and actions as immoral or otherwise but, as the narrative proceeds, reversals take

[11] Generalizing from the ascetic and erotic aspects of the mythology of Shiva, O'Flaherty (1975: 315) writes: 'The ancient Indian knew well the Faustian lust for the full experience of the most diverse possibilities of human life; the Buddha saw this thirst as the cause of all human misery but the Hindus did not dismiss it so easily. They recognized a constant tension between the desire to sample every aspect of experience and the desire to exhaust at least one by plumbing its depths. Thus every human action involves a choice, and every choice implies a loss.' I am struck by this author's attempt to oppose the Western tendency of forcing a choice between opposites to the Hindu's willingness to live with dualities; it seems to me that she underplays the problem of levels and the importance of transcendence, which of course is not synthesis, for the Hindu. This could hardly be explained adequately by citing her preoccupation with mythology rather than metaphysics, for the two are not unrelated in Hindu thought.

place and each crucial character is transformed into the opposite type, with the very notable exception of Kach in *Yayati*, who is an embodiment of the wisdom of transcendentalism. Thus, the opposition between Kumaragiri and Bijagupta, between Praneshacharya and Naranappa, and somewhat less dramatically between Yati and Yayati, is sustained from the beginning to the bitter end through this process of inversion. The option for devotion to spiritual pursuits, that is, for asceticism, which may at first blush appear good and laudable, leads each seeker to his own particular experience of disastrous and painful failure.

Kumaragiri, whose worst faults are his preoccupation with himself, his egotism (*ahaṁkāra*), falls so low indeed that he resorts to deceit to satisfy his aroused erotic desires. While his life lies in ruins, Bijagupta emerges as the true renouncer, because he has always been one through his concern for others. Similarly, Praneshacharya seeks merit and god through a well-regulated life—though a householder, he is an ascetic—only to discover its emptiness. This leads him to suspect, if not believe, that Naranappa, the voluptuary who flouted all rules, may after all have been the one to find god. Yati, too, sets out to discover god but all he finds is loneliness, thorns and bitter fruit, and ends up being a deranged person. Yayati, on the other hand, draws up the programme of his life in terms of the pursuit of pleasure and comes to grief. Both of them have to be taught the lesson of the importance of harmonization of opposites, and the moral arrogance (or stupidity) of either/or choices.

The trap of binary oppositions is everybody's misfortune. While Kumaragiri and Bijagupta are Brahman and Kshatriya respectively, Praneshacharya and Naranappa are both Brahmans of the same sect, and Yati and Yayati are even closer, brothers sharing common substance. The victim carries no prior mark other than his humanity. By questioning commonly accepted moral judgements, such as the one which places high value on asceticism and denigrates eroticism, the discourses create what may be called 'moral suspense' or 'moral perplexity'. If the option which is obviously good is not in fact so, how then does one make one's moral choices? Three solutions to this problem are suggested in the novels.

Chitralekha takes the stand that all choices are a snare, that dualities are an illusion, and that one must therefore seek a state of consciousness in which one's vision is so enlarged that one is able to rise above the domain of choice-making. The situations in which human beings are placed in worldly life are far more powerful than they. This realization must not be allowed to lead to quietism or, worse, nihilism. The wise do not seek merit through moral choices of the either/or kind, but through transcendence, which is not the same as synthesis. Morality is not an external condition, a mere attribute of human conduct, but an inner wisdom, a mental stage, from which all our acts should flow naturally without an effort of will.[12]

The second solution, which is perhaps better described as an 'anti-solution', is provided in *Samskara*. The man who will follow where his bodily appetites lead him is no more a thing blown around in the wind than the man who lives by mechanically-learnt rules. Both deny that the essence of human life lies in its possibilities. It is therefore not the kind of life one leads that is so important to a person's moral stature as the consciousness of purpose and procedure that he or she is able to bring into it. As Jung would put it, the way to personal truth may lie only through an inferno of passions. This is why Naranappa may have been touched by God but Praneshacharya was not.

The human being as a fully conscious or autonomous moral agent (a Socrates-like figure) is, then, the ideal *Samskara* puts forward; but it is an ideal difficult to realize, for no human being living in society may hope to make all his or her own choices without taking away from the autonomy of others. Moral choices thus generate moral dilemmas with no easy solutions. Perhaps exceptionally gifted persons such as the ancient sages, whom one may call moral heroes, were able to solve this problem by learning to transcend dualities, including the opposition between cultural determination and free will, but what about ordinary people? Like Praneshacharya, they may only wait—anxious, expectant.

[12] Such a 'mental state' may well appear as a regrettable condition in another cultural tradition. Thus: 'There is a kind of disease of thinking which always looks for (and finds) what would be called a mental state from which all our facts spring as from a reservoir (Wittgenstein 1964: 143).

Yayati introduces into this discussion a third solution. It begins with the idealist argument, namely that morality is tied up with one's station in life and its attendant duties. This is rather like the formulation about 'situations' in *Chitralekha*. Moral choices, according to this argument, are socially given and, therefore, known, They are summed up in the *dharma* appropriate to one's social group (*varṇa*), stage of life (*āśrama*), place (*sthāna*) and time (*kāla*). Thus the householder must live by the morality of *puruṣārtha*, as given in the three values (*tri-varga*) of *dharma*, *artha* and *kāma*. A harmonious structuring in hierarchical complementarity of the activities that these values betoken, with *dharma* encompassing *artha* and *kāma*, is the recommended moral choice for the man-in-the-world.[13] Though none of the three novels is about the life of the householder (Praneshacharya with his world-view and the invalid, childless wife is and yet is not one), *gārhasthya* as a moral condition emerges at the centre of the discourses, though only by implication. The householder combines in himself, and mediates between, both the ascetic and the erotic ideals. In this lies his cultural significance.

It is important to note that the foregoing solution of harmonization of opposites is not quite the same as Aristotle's notion of the 'golden mean', nor is it an effort to arrive at a simple synthesis. Neither should it be confused with the various projects of the neo-Freudians to restore dignity to the human body (Brown 1959), to bring love and reason together (Bettelheim 1961), or to strive for autonomy, the assertion of individuality and the practice of the common good (Arieti 1972). Similarly, it should be distinguished from the contemporary anthropological effort to underscore the cultural construction of nature, including the human body (see, e.g., Schneider 1968). Important though these approaches to the resolution of the nature–culture opposition are, they are meaningful primarily within Western philosophical traditions. The harmonization of opposites mentioned in *Yayati* is related, rather, to the

[13] Cf: 'There are three "human ends", *dharma*, *artha* and *kāma*, duty, profit and pleasure. All three are (necessary and) lawful, but they are so graded in a hierarchy that an inferior ideal may be pursued only as far as a superior one does not intervene: *dharma* . . . is more important than *artha* . . . which, in turn, is above *kāma* . . .' (Dumont 1960: 41). Also see above, fn. 12 on p. 33.

other solution, namely transcendence, proposed for the sannyasi: *the former is, in fact, a step leading to the latter*, and it is important to emphasize this fact.

Transcendence is a complex concept and, it seems to me, much misunderstood. Following the clues available in *Yayati*, and developing them, it could be said to refer to raising the level of being in order to free it from the conflict of dualities. This is the ancient goal (rather than object) of *saṁskṛti*, the bringing into being of the mature, refined person. Nothing is discarded or excluded in this process of refinement: everything is included, improved and carried forward into one integrated experience. In this experience eroticism exists no more nor less than does asceticism. The goal is to connect them, to establish a proper relationship between them. The relationship alone is real in the same sense in which the truth of the trader's balance lies in the even beam and not in either of the two pans or their contents.

Transcendence, then, bestows on one the holistic vision that sees all in terms of mutual relatedness in a framework of values. It thus frees the human being from the need to make choices. The duality between the householder and the renouncer, suggested in *Yayati*, is also dissolved, as, according to the notion of *āśrama*, every *gṛhastha* is ultimately expected to become a sannyasi. It is in this sense that renunciation is, as Dumont so aptly calls it, 'a sort of universal language in India' (1970: 52). *Yayati* thus upholds the notion of transcendence as the supreme value in the moral domain, and suggests a solution to the ethical relativism of *Chitralekha* and the existentialist's agonizing, his trembling in the face of choice-making, so poignantly portrayed in *Samskara*.[14]

The three discourses discussed here contain a number of bipolar concepts which are all apparently transformations of the basic opposition between nature and culture. Thus, there are conceptualizations of biopsychological states (body–soul/spirit, youth–old age, woman–man, madness/folly–sanity/wisdom, pleasure–joy, pleasure–pain), of social types (householder/king–sannyasi, prostitute–wife, *bhogī–yogī*), of human conduct (eroti-

[14] It is indeed puzzling that Carl Jung (1977: 306) should have thought that the condition of *nirdvandva* does not refer to moral perfection. This underscores the whole issue of the problems of cross-cultural communication.

cism–asceticism, acceptance of worldly goals–renunciation, search for knowledge through experience–quest for intuitive knowledge), and of moral values (*pāpa–puṇya*, *nīti–dharma*, life affirmation–life denial). Whereas a correspondence between biopsychological states, social types and modes of conduct may be readily established, doing the same between these, on the one hand, and the moral value pairs, on the other, is problematic. Thus it is a woman, and significantly a woman living outside the rules of society, a Chitralekha or a Chandri, who becomes the instrument employed to reclaim ascetics like Kumaragiri and Praneshacharya for the domain of nature. Such a woman is supposed to live in sin but, judging by the turn of events in the novels, does she really? Yayati is, of course, a king and not a sannyasi: even in his spiritual evolution it is not his queen but 'the other woman', Sharmishtha, who plays the crucial positive role. Looked at in this way, the discourses, once again, point to the importance of transcendence, of perceiving nature and culture as a unity.[15]

The above discussion suggests, I think, that the anthropological study of moral choices in South Asian societies will be enriched if it is carried out in the light of native categories of thought. Such categories do not, of course, provide the anthropologist with readymade answers, but without them he himself may not give any that are significant. Moreover, such an approach will generate insights into people's observable behaviour which may lead to conclusions about it that are significantly different from those flowing from a Eurocentric view of moral choices. Some students of comparative philosophy have already noted that the ultimate concern of the Hindu is not

[15] Ramanujan rightly remarks in the Translator's Note that, '*Samskara* takes its title seriously'; he translates it as 'a rite for a dead man' in the context of the novel. I would prefer to emphasize, in the context of this essay, that other first meaning of the word *samskara* which, quoting from the epigraph provided by Ramanujan, refers to the 'forming well or thoroughly, making perfect' of human beings. *Samskara* goes with *saṁskṛiti* (culture) as opposed to *prakṛiti* (nature). It points to the process of maturation, of moral perfectibility.

Some readers may wonder if *Samskara* is really comparable to *Chitralekha* and *Yayati* in view of the influence of Western philosophy and literature on Anantha Murthy. I am not too bothered about this because, for one thing, his novel is a modern Hindu intellectual's work and, secondly, the experience of existentialist distress has not been unknown to Indian thinkers.

with choice, which is imprisonment, but with freedom (Potter 1963: 1–24 *et passim*).[16] Far from implying a rejection of Western philosophical traditions as irrelevant because they are external, or an acceptance of Indian philosophical traditions as sufficient because they are internal, this essay is an effort to reaffirm the dialectical nature of anthropological knowledge.

[16] See the Introduction for the Indian philosopher J. Krishnamurti's statement of the notion of freedom from choice-making.

4
THE DESIRED AND THE GOOD

. . . it is well for him who takes hold of the 'good', but he who chooses the 'desired' fails in his aim.

KATHA UPANISHAD

As you would not like to change something very beautiful . . . so do not put obstacles in the way of suffering. Allow it to ripen, for with its flowering understanding comes.

J. KRISHNAMURTI

In the course of studying the Pandits of Kashmir I have detected among them an abiding concern with the problem of suffering (*duḥkha*). While suffering has a physical aspect, it is its mental and emotional aspects which are emphasized by them. Everyday speech is replete with references to the varieties of suffering which the Pandits consider to be the lot of humankind. Though they bemoan its wide prevalence, and express bewilderment in respect of particular cases, they do not consider suffering in general as ununderstandable, for they subscribe to the notion of the 'fruits of action' (*karma-phala*): one deserves what one gets in life, no matter how deep the suffering. While there is much mutual sympathy, there is also the exhortation that one should submit to suffering in a spirit of resignation, seek to ensure a better future through righteousness of thought and action, and leave the rest to divine blessing (*anugraha*).

Given the concern with human suffering, which the Pandits doubtless share with peoples everywhere, they also expatiate on the causes of it. These are seen as being multiple and, indeed, as belonging to different ontological levels. Generally speaking, suffering is considered to be the result of wrong actions which, in turn, may be traced to a moral infirmity of some kind. Ultimately, however, wrong-doing is believed to result from ignorance and delusion (*moha-māyā*) and egotism (*ahaṁkāra*). The individual sufferer is, therefore, always exhorted to improve his understanding of the true nature of things and happenings and, above all, of his own *potential for goodness*. The divine is immanent in the human, the Pandits aver; in fact, he who attains moral perfection knows that he is divine. It is not, however, given to everyone to attain such perfection. It requires ceaseless endeavour directed towards self-improvement (maturation) and is ultimately a divine gift.

The call to make choices in ordering one's life in terms of what are generally acknowledged in Pandit culture as moral imperatives is not an occasional challenge, therefore, but an everyday responsibility for most people. A well-known guide to the making of the right choices is the Upanishadic dichotomy of the 'desired' (*preyas*) and the 'good' (*śreyas*). As the Pandits see it, the pursuit of worldly gains and pleasures—of *artha* and *kāma*—is perfectly legitimate provided it is carried out in accordance with righteousness (*dharma*). In other words, the 'desired' and the 'good' are not to be opposed to each other but integrated in an enlarged moral sensibility. *Preyas* must be brought under the sovereignty of *śreyas*, and *śreyas* may be realized through an affirmation of worldly goals and not necessarily through their denial. The Pandit ideology of the householder gives expression to such a view of the good life.[1]

At the highest level of moral discipline, or spiritual endeavour, there is the Brahmanical ideal of the final ending of ignorance (*avidyā*) through attaining the state of transcendence in life. One who attains such a level of human perfection does not suffer from the agony of having to face moral dilemmas; he is freed from having to make choices. For such a self-aware person, the goal is the joy (*ānanda*) of *being* good rather than seeking *to become* good. In the words of the well-known contemporary philosopher, J. Krishnamurti, such a person lives in 'choiceless awareness'.[2]

But how many ordinary people, ask the Pandits, may hope to attain such perfection (*siddhi*)? They see most human lives as tales of moral infirmity, some more so than others. Those who are found wanting in moral virtue are not, however, left without hope. 'Nobody goes astray for ever': this maxim is

[1] See Chapter 2. [2] See above, p. 13.

said to be one of the basic truths of human existence. A person can and should try to repair the damaged moral fabric of his life but the mode of atonement (*prāyaścitta*) varies from person to person. Cultural injunctions do not bind the moral agent absolutely, nor is there scope for full freedom or originality in a person's response to his predicament. These variations in modes of atonement tell us more about the 'moral space' available within one's culture than about individual idiosyncrasies.

Wrong-doing does not, of course, take place in a social vacuum: interpersonal relations of the most intimate kind—such as those between wife and husband or parent and child—are their principal locus. In fact, it is in the context of such primal settings that the agony of choice-making comes out most explicitly and poignantly, for these relations are seen by the Pandits as being governed by moral imperatives rather than being subject to human choice. Moreover, different degrees of wrong-doing are recognized, ranging from the ordinarily faulty actions (*aparādha*, *doṣa*) to those which are judged as morally reprehensible and evil (*pāpa*). The nature and extent of the effort needed to restore the moral balance of one's life is understandably seen as being dependent upon the magnitude of one's lapse.

What is true of the Pandits is likely to be broadly true of other Brahman communities also. In this chapter I explore further some of the ideas presented above very briefly, by drawing upon the insights provided by a contemporary Tamil novel about a south Indian Brahman community. I hasten to add that, apart from some very minor details, the Pandits would, in my judgement, find nothing in this novel—no incident and no moral judgement—lying outside the range of possibility in their own midst. I have chosen T. Janakiraman's *The Sins of Appu's Mother*[3] rather than an ethnographic text, because it deals with certain kinds of moral issues which have not been

[3] The original title of the novel, *Amma Vantal*, would read 'Mother came' in English. It is noteworthy that it is not Janakiraman but the translator, M. Krishnan, who emphasizes the word 'sin' by putting it into the title of the novel. I have been told by the novelist's daughter, Uma Shankari, that, as far as she knows, the novelist was on the whole satisfied with the translation. A. K. Ramanujan tells me, however, that the translation leaves much to be desired.

taken up for study by sociologists or anthropologists in India. The reason for this lacuna in ethnographic literature may well be that such moral issues and the choices they entail are not readily available to the scrutiny of the student who would seek to understand them only from without—as behaviour, perhaps —independent of the cultural constructs of the people which embody thought and feeling. This is not to deny the existence and importance of cross-cultural moral imperatives, but to stress that such 'universals' must necessarily be experienced as 'particulars' by the actors. And the ethnographic method encourages us to concentrate on the moral acts of a people when we would seek to explicate the notion of morality in their culture.

Turning to the novel, then, we learn that Appu is his mother's third and last legitimate child. Alankaram—for that is her name—has three other children, but their father is not the same as Appu's, namely Dandapani, but a client of his called Shivasu. Dandapani is an astrologer and a scholar of ancient texts. He is a nondescript Brahman who makes a living as a proof-reader in a printing press and by teaching Sanskrit texts to elderly and retired city gentlemen. He lives a humdrum life with his wife and children in a tenement situated in a lane in Madras. Performing ablutions, offering prayers, eating, and working—these appear to be the activities that consume him, just as they constitute the everyday life of most Brahmans everywhere. In his youth he too had known conjugal pleasures, but these had later been taken away from him irrevocably by Alankaram, who preferred Shivasu; and Dandapani chose to put up with this liaison and the children born of it. She had made a culturally forbidden choice and he had acquiesced in it. Both acted stealthily and in bad conscience, for neither questioned the cultural norms in the light of which they were wrong-doers.

Unlike her husband, Alankaram is a rather extraordinary character, aptly named Alankaram, for the word means 'ornament'. Somehow, muses Dandapani on one occasion after discovering her perfidy, her parents had not given her the name of a Hindu goddess, which is the common practice among orthodox Brahmans, but one more like that of a courtesan.

Alankaram is a tall, well-built, physically attractive woman, and, though not well-read, a person of imagination and a strong will. There is a touch of the arrogant and even the regal about her, and she dominates the scene wherever she is by her natural grace and poise.

She sat majestically in her chair, in that tenement, in that cattle-yard lane, like a queen on her throne. In her smile and speech and the way she turned and walked she was regal. She never pleaded and she never bargained. And she never spoke at needless length. (p. 102)

She would look in wonder at the stars and see in their constellations shapes that he could never make out clearly, no matter how explicitly she pointed them out [to Dandapani, lying beside her on the terrace of their house]. There was something childlike in her wonder at the stars, the shapes she could see in them, even in the way she lay still on her back staring at them. . . . It was not only her star-gazing; her dreams too were extraordinary; vivid, colourful and detailed. They were peopled by strange characters and beings and mythological figures with everything larger than life. His own dreams seemed so mundane and poverty-stricken by comparison . . . (p.72)

Appu was Alankaram's favourite child and she paid special attention to his upbringing. When he was eight years old, and in school, Alankaram revealed to her husband her 'deep wish to give him a real education' (p. 75). Dandapani agreed and spoke of Appu going to the university and perhaps becoming a teacher or an engineer, but she dismissed such ideas as commonplace.

He must learn the Vedas. He must study them intensely and shine with their effulgence. Like fire he should burn up all pettiness and dross that come near him and should stand like a god; like Brihaspati. (p. 76)[4]

Dandapani's pleas that a Vedic scholar cannot hope to make a decent living are brushed aside. Appu can acquire a more utilitarian education later on—but first the Vedas. Sixteen years later, Appu, an adept in Vedic scholarship, back from the village where he studied the sacred texts and looking for work to do, expresses his own doubts about the self-sufficiency of such knowledge. Alankaram admonishes him in reply:

[4] Brihaspati is the preceptor, counsellor, and chief priest of the Vedic gods.

If one reads the Vedas one's mind and body are purified and acquire an effulgence. No illness or anxiety can touch such a person, for he becomes like a flower—an undying, ever fresh flower. . . . Nobody will let a [Vedic scholar become just a mean, beggarly priest]. Don't go grubbing for money and your study will look after you. (pp. 102–3)

This high idealism and faith in the Vedas are, in fact, also a cover for a very personal motive. Having chosen the life of pleasure (*kāma*, *preyas*), outside the framework of righteous conduct (*dharma*)—there is no higher mode of righteousness for the Brahman wife than conjugal fidelity, for then she becomes a *pativratā* ('sworn to her husband'), spiritually mightier than even the goddesses—Alankaram had obviously felt driven by her conscience to choose a way to atone for her sin: she had decided to make Appu a Vedic scholar. As she confesses to him when he prepares to return to the village on hearing that the old woman who had provided him both home and school during the sixteen years of his Vedic studies is ill (Alankaram is afraid Appu will not come back to her):

You are someone very special to me, Appu. It is by my concern for you that I must atone for everything. You are my last son. [She repudiates the three illegitimate children.] I tortured myself thinking how I could find atonement. Violent suicide could only mean my death and the end of me. Finally I decided to put you into the *pathshala* [traditional Brahmanical school]. Those who learn the Vedas become *rishis* [singers of sacred hymns, sages]. They are ageless and pure as fire. I hoped you would return like that and I could fall at your feet . . . (p. 123)

Alankaram had hoped to atone for her moral lapse by ensuring the moral perfection of her son and then serving him and thus become herself purified. She made her choices selfishly and, therefore, they were not wise: neither when she preferred Shivasu over Dandapani nor when she preferred Apu over her other children. Not that a parent in upper-caste Hindu society would be blamed for dedicating one of the sons to the study of the Vedas; but her choice of the life of a Vedic scholar for her son had been tainted by her primary concern with her own atonement. A son is by definition the saviour, *putra*, one who delivers his parents and ancestors from the tortures of hell.[5] This obligation is an absolute value: the essence of sonship is filial piety. But when an errant mother (or father) looks upon the son as the instrument of her (or his) salvation, the relationship becomes perverted and the parental purpose defeated.

Appu does indeed decide to stay on in the village. He is repelled by a morally amorphous city—'I don't like anything about Madras' (p. 147)—and from a home where he has suffered the most grievous emotional trauma that a son may have to experience—the painful discovery that both his mother and father must be judged by him to be morally infirm. Alankaram's arrogance and Dandapani's cowardice weigh the same ultimately in the scale of moral values. On his return from the village school after a sixteen-year absence, Appu's discovery of Alankaram's truth made him see her in a new light. 'Why could she not be ordinary, like other people's mothers? Why did she have this imperious bearing and form, this arrogance on her face? . . .' (p. 109). As for Dandapani, 'Why did he not leave the house and become a sanyasi? Why was he still eating the food she cooked and served, indifferent to disgrace?' (p. 114). Appu had indeed wanted to tell his father: 'I feel like crying when I look at you. Do you call yourself a man? . . . I feel you ought to be driven away from home' (p. 117). In putting up with a wife who was unfaithful to him, Dandapani was unfaithful to his own truly begotten children.

Realizing that Appu would not come home, Alankaram visits him in the village, only to have her fears confirmed: he is not going back, for there is no 'home' to go back to—just a house. The home is a moral place marked by conjugal fidelity and filial piety. She must now make her *final* choice, which she does, firmly as before, but this time wisely. She tells Appu she is going north, far from Madras, to the sacred city of Kashi, to await her death there.

[5] *Naraka*, hell, is a place for the torture for sinners and for those whose post-mortuary rites have not been performed properly. There are a number of *narakas*, and *put* is one of them. The deliverance of those consigned to hell for want of post-mortuary rites, and prevention of one's manes (*pitṛ*) being so condemned, is achieved through oblations, particularly the biannual food offerings called *śrāddha*. The person who makes these food offerings is *ideally* one's natural son, but there are others who are also eligible to do so.

It is sound sense [she says]. A woman must die in front of her son—or in Kashi. I thought of you as my only son [she actually had three] and I thought you had become a *rishi* and at your feet I hoped to burn my soul; my all. But you have become a mother's son [the reference is to the benefactress of the village Vedic school]. . . . I am going to Kashi and live there. . . . There is no other way. Many old women go to Kashi to die. I, too, shall go there and wait. (p. 165)

It may be pointed out here that, in conformity with traditional Hindu belief, Alankaram might have expressed the wish to die at the feet of her husband, but she treats him as if he were dead by proposing to act as Hindu widows do. She has wronged him but she will not seek his forgiveness. The novelist clearly suggests that she is a culturally abnormal person. Only widows go to die in Kashi: it is a common belief that a widow must have been guilty of some moral lapse and her widowhood is punishment for that. Dying in Kashi not only absolves one of all sins but—and this is so much more significant from the Hindu point of view—also ensures *mokṣa*, liberation from rebirth through union with the Absolute. This becomes possible as God grants knowledge to the devotee at the very moment of his or her death in Kashi, destroying the fruits of all past actions—good and bad (see Parry 1981).

So Alankaram goes to Kashi: her pursuit of *kāma* (eros) entails for her the pursuit of *kāla* (thanatos). Or shall we say that she goes there to begin a new life, as an autonomous moral agent, cutting off all her worldly attachments, including the bond with her favourite son? It might be argued here that without worldly attachments there is nothing to be moral about, but the novelist seems more interested in highlighting yet another and more general strand in Hindu thought. Alankaram will now be her own saviour by her act of renunciation and through divine grace. When taking leave of the school benefactress (who had called Appu back to the village), Alankaram had sought her blessing so that she might gain 'knowledge and enlightenment'. The old lady had assured her: 'God will give everything. If one abandons oneself to Him, there is nothing he will not give' (p. 164).

Turning now to Appu, we find that he had met and known two women at the village Vedic school—its benefactress, Bhavaniammal, and her brother's daughter, Indu, who is a few months younger than Appu. Finding herself a childless widow at thirty, but in possession of an estate in land, Bhavaniammal had endowed most of it to establish the school. She had brought her brother there to teach and Indu was his daughter. His wife and he had died within a couple of years of each other, leaving the little Indu an orphan. Bhavaniammal arranged Indu's marriage, but her husband also died three years later. Appu had arrived at the school before Indu's marriage and Bhavaniammal had thus been a foster mother to both the boy and the girl.

When Appu is grappling with the painful situation in his home, after having returned there on the completion of his studies—in acknowledgement of his familial obligation about which his father had kept reminding him—Bhavaniammal suffers from a paralytic stroke. Informed about it, Appu rushes back to the village. Though Bhavaniammal is out of danger by the time he gets there, she is not sure of the future. Besides, the old teacher in the school, who had taken her brother's place, is also not well. Bhavaniammal had, in fact, asked Appu to stay on to teach when he finished his studies, but he declined, even though the village school had been like a home to him. She now repeats her invitation and Appu accepts, disillusioned as he is with his own home and parents.

Bhavaniammal is a very humane and practical woman. Her 'mind is like the Kaveri [which flows beside the village]. It rolls along broad and majestic, with affection and compassion in its swell' (p. 153). She gets the land deed altered to ensure that Appu and Indu will be provided for, even if no more pupils come to learn the Vedas. She is afraid that many villagers will be jealous of Appu and that the orthodox among them will not approve of Appu living under the same roof as the young widow; Bhavaniammal surely knows that Indu and Appu have always been in love with each other. And yet she alters her will in their favour because, as she says, her affection for the two of them is greater than her reverence for the Vedas—a very bold confession for a Brahman woman to make. She recalls that she had endowed the school thirty years earlier to enable some people to learn the Vedas—and one hundred and four pupils had done so already.

[But] why count the heads? Is that not mere pride? The Vedas will survive even without us. They are eternal. . . . If you [Appu] can, continue to teach the Vedas. And if you cannot, give food and shelter to a few boys, then send them to some Tamil or English school. Let them have a free choice. What does it matter whether one learns the Vedas or something else? A few boys who are destitute must be fed. But it is necessary to be aware of god and he is there in the shape of hunger. If you remember that for my sake, it shall be sufficient (pp. 148–9).

Bhavaniammal's view of the world is a balanced one, neither thoughtlessly conventional nor sentimental. Her primary concern appears to be the good of others—be they Indu, Appu, or the village children. She is Appu's second mother, as it were, and Alankaram realizes this when she visits the village in the hope of claiming back her son, and learns of what Bhavaniammal has done. Alankaram's love for Appu and the choice she made on his behalf were rooted in concern for herself—her pursuit of pleasure and the wish to atone for her sins both stemmed from this preoccupation. There is, however, sarcasm as well as sorrow in Alankaram's speech when she tells Appu that he has become 'a mother's son' instead of a sage and seer (*ṛṣi*). The reference is to his supposed fall, for she implies that he has been ensnared by Bhavaniammal's will. Alankaram had hoped that he would be free of worldly entanglements—that, himself redeemed by the Vedas, he would deliver others from sin and the bitter fruits of sin.

It seems to me that in this story Bhavaniammal alone emerges unsullied by any self-centred involvement with mundane affairs. She lives for others and uses her worldly possessions for their good and happiness. She cares for them for their own sake; she loves Appu for his own sake first and only then for the sake of the Vedas. She is the mother who gives and does not demand; she makes her choices wisely and is a *true* mother. Though a widow, she by no means betokens inauspiciousness. Like women-*bhakta* (devotees of god), she has cast away her human husband to devote herself to god's creatures and traversed half the way to divinity. The contrast with the casting away of Dandapani by Alankaram is striking, in both its manner and significance.

Human mothers may be foolish or wise but motherhood remains a supreme value in Hindu thought. In the myths and symbols of Hindu civilization, bountiful, nourishing motherhood is represented by rivers; in Janakiraman's novel it is represented by the Kaveri.[6] In fact, when Appu tells Indu that Bhavaniammal is affectionate and compassionate, he compares her to the Kaveri's broad and majestic roll. Significantly, the reader is introduced to the Kaveri even before he is introduced to Appu or anybody else in the opening paragraph of the novel, which speaks of his having become possessed by the river during his sixteen years in the village on its banks.

Appu had been frightened by his first encounter with the Kaveri the morning after his arrival in the village, when his father took him to its banks for a bath. The river was in flood, turbulent, rolling by like 'some great sighing snake' (p. 6). On that very first encounter we had also had a sight of the bounty of the river: a kingfisher plunging for its prey and emerging with something in its beak. Ever afterwards, Appu had found a mother in the Kaveri in whom he could confide—to whom 'he could speak his heart' (p. 150), and then listen. While his Vedic teacher taught him to sing the hymns and recite the texts loud and clear, perhaps bending his ear to detect and correct any mispronunciation, the Kaveri taught him to listen and speak in silence: but it spoke to him of the same truth as the Vedas—of the Eternal and the Absolute. When Bhavaniammal tells Appu that she has altered her will and what she envisages the future might be like, he makes

> his way to the Kaveri—whatever emotion moved him it was always, and only, to the river that he could speak his heart. . . . He remembered the evening he had come here just after finishing his studies, shortly before leaving for home. Today he felt just as he had that day—a sense of seeing the river anew and a strong reluctance to go away from it. (pp. 150–1)

There is a kind of mysterious primary bond of attachment

[6] After I had written this essay, I came across the following observation about the villagers of Kumbapettai in the Thanjavur district of Tamilnadu: 'The river Kaveri and its irrigation channels were thought of as the villagers' mother. The muddy water in mid-July was her menstruation, the flood tide in early August her pregnancy, and the harvest her children' (Gough 1981: 170; also see ibid.: 225–6). A. K. Ramanujan tells me that T. Janakiraman wrote a book on the Kaveri.

between Appu and the Kaveri—like that of a child to its mother, rooted in the depths of his being, but finding in culture the tongue with which to express it. It is noteworthy that not only do we take leave of Appu in the village on the bank of the Kaveri—the Ganga of the South, so called—we also remember that Alankaram is on her way to Kashi to live and die on the bank of the Ganga itself—the holiest of India's rivers. According to Hindu tradition, these holy rivers of India wash away not only human sins but also the imperfections of being and understanding that necessitate the making of choices.[7] Though an elemental part of nature, the river here emerges as a key symbol for culture, while Alankaram, by an interesting reversal, symbolizes nature in the form of rampant human appetites. Bhavaniammal bridges nature and culture and points to the human potential for moral perfection. Though human like Alankaram, she is more like the Kaveri in her bounteousness.

Appu remains unfree—or so it seems to me—as his choices are made for him by others, though he does not abide by all of them. Alankaram's choice makes him a Vedic scholar, but he alone could have made himself a *ṛṣi*. His father's exhortations bring him home from the village—a father who, he comes to believe in the end, should himself have been driven away from home—but he alone could have chosen to become a householder (*gṛhastha*). Bhavaniammal recalls him to the village, involving him in an act of renunciation, but he alone may will it. He resists Indu's love, believing that he is expected by his culture and society to treat another man's wife or widow as his mother or sister, but this moral position also he finds difficult to sustain. He has to confess to himself that he has always been in love with Indu without having had the courage to admit it. In fact, he had rebuked Indu for declaring her love for him and beseeching him not to go away on the eve of his departure from the village, on completion of his studies. He had told her that her face reminded him of his mother's,

[7] The rich symbolism of the redeeming rivers (and rain) is familiar to students of Hindu ritual, mythology, art and architecture. It has also found its way into contemporary fiction. A notable example is Herman Hesse's fine novel *Siddhartha*, which is not only about India but, more significantly, about 'the quest and yearning of nature for new forms and new possibilities'.

that he hoped to go back to his mother 'clean in body and clean in mind'—an adept in the Vedas—without 'smearing' himself with the 'mud' of an illegitimate erotic relationship. 'When you return after a bath in the holy Kaveri you shouldn't drop into a roadside tavern' (p. 42). His final, pathetic appeal to her had been: 'Send me home safe'. And home he went as a dutiful son, only to discover the bitter truth about his mother and father, which turns him into a mildly rebellious son.

Finally, on his return to the village, having yielded to Bhavaniammal's persuasion to stay on, Appu meekly accepts Indu's invitation to share his burdens with her—which is itself not a clear choice, only an acquiescence: 'if ever anything bothers you, tell it to me whatever it is. You can't bear it alone . . .' (p. 143). What could the sharing of burdens between them mean, for Brahman widows do not remarry? In this sense, though the novel ends, the moral discourse contained in it does not come to a satisfactory conclusion. Appu's moral dilemmas—arising out of his relations with the three women in his life—remain unresolved. In opting to live in the village with Indu, does he really surrender to Alankaram? Does his decision never to marry, conveyed to Alankaram during her fateful visit to the village, constitute a vow of celibacy? If so, will he have the moral courage to adhere to it in the presence of Indu's searing passion for him? Already, before the story is brought to its end, Appu seems to have overcome his earlier resistance to being even touched by Indu. When she first declared her love for him, he had sought to silence her by pronouncing physical love between them as sinful. Her retort had been: 'It doesn't seem to me. What is a sin? To do and say things against one's conscience' (p. 40). Appu had no answer to that; obviously Indu's view of moral conduct is different from everybody else's in the novel.

Indu appears to be the only character who repudiates cultural norms, not guiltily as Alankaram does, but innocently and even self-confidently. She appeals to a higher morality than that of culture—the morality of conscience. But this remains regrettably vague in the novel. I would not disagree with the novelist if he wants to suggest that honesty with one's own self-authenticity is the cornerstone of morality; but there appears to be a crucial difference between the honesty of Bhavaniammal and Indu. While the former judges what she feels in terms of the good of others, even if it is unconventional, the latter's stand seems to point to the idealization of the intensity of feeling—and this could turn out to be a perilous path, thin and sharp as the proverbial razor's edge.[8]

Appu perhaps never listened carefully enough to the Kaveri, which would have liberated him, but only to the human mothers who bind him to the wheel of *karma*. Bhavaniammal, the 'good' mother, does this no less than Alankaram, the 'bad' mother. In fact, the former binds him fast to this world in a three-stranded bond of attachment (like the three-stranded holy neck cord symbolizing a Brahman's worldly obligations) consisting of the land, the school, and Indu. The flowing river would have spoken to Appu of the Brahmanical quest for the dissolution of worldly attachments and obligations and the supreme value of transcendence in the context of moral choices. The ideal is to overcome the agony of making choices by attaining a level of self-awareness which enables one to act morally as a matter of course—spontaneously.

To conclude: human beings live in socially constructed worlds, and everywhere the *nomos* is legitimated in terms of, among other values, certain moral imperatives. The social order thus becomes a cosmo-moral order. This fact does not, however, render it immune to the unsettling impact of human choices which question, seek to alter, or even repudiate its moral foundations. Not to speak of other social relationships, even the universally acknowledged 'axiomatic amity' (Fortes 1969) of the mother–son relationship may turn out to be fragile, as it indeed does in the case of Alankaram and Appu. Though one does not choose one's parents or, in traditional Brahman communities, one's spouse,[9] a person may still be faced with situations involving choice between alternative modes of relating

[8] The clash of *dharmas* and the opposition of culture and conscience is a perennial theme of Hindu culture. One of its most celebrated expressions is in the constant self-questioning of Yudhishthira, the very embodiment of *dharma* in the Mahabharata. In our own times, Gandhi's life is a similar notable example.

[9] I do not have in mind only the prescriptive marriage (with a cousin) in south India, but also the widespread practice of parent-arranged marriage in Hindu society.

to them. If these choices are not made wisely, they result in suffering.

The Sins of Appu's Mother may be read as a discourse on the making of moral choices and the suffering or contentment (if not fulfilment) that they bring to the moral agent. This may be highlighted by recapitulating the choices that the major characters in the novel make, their individual experience of suffering, and the manner in which they cope with it.

Shivasu is a shadowy figure and, from the little one is able to gather about him, he could well be the typical amoral person for whom the distinction between good and bad choices is meaningless. His sole concern is with the pursuit of pleasure, unmindful of any norms, so that the 'desired' (*preyas*) is judged to be good in itself without reference to a higher and encompassing notion of the 'good' (*sreyas*). Dandapani, in contrast, is a weak character who suffers, one presumes, from his wife's rejection of him as husband and mentor, from her fall from the ideal of chastity, as also, perhaps, from his own helplessness. 'One must not try too hard to understand. Keep quiet, just looking on [he tells Appu]. That's what God has created us for' (p. 118). He obviously keeps his suffering to himself, and finds consolation in the many mundane chores of his daily life. He may be mistaken for a renouncer but he seems to be only a compromiser who settles for life in a shrunken moral space.[10]

Both Shivasu and Dandapani are dominated by Alankaram. One gets the impression that she could have rejected Shivasu, just as she had discarded Dandapani, but that she chooses not to do so till the very end. When she calls Shivasu 'the serpent that circled my feet' (p. 124) in her last conversation with Appu before he finally leaves home, she basically covers up or mistakes her own pleasure-seeking self for her lover. Alankaram is an abnormally demanding person and the choices she makes bring suffering to her and to others, and lead her almost inevitably to seek a tryst with death—a choice beyond which there are no more choices to make in this life. Her suffering arises from a sense of moral rectitude, however. Unlike Shivasu, she seems to be aware of the distinction between the 'desired'

[10] Uma Shankari (Janakiraman's daughter) holds that Dandapani's resignation is a form of renunciation and that he has in a sense come close to being a detached person. I do not quite see him in that light (personal communication).

and the 'good': only her path to the latter ideal lies for her through repentance for an exclusive pursuit of the former. The story of her life and the choices that constitute it, including the final renunciation, reveal her to be a morally infirm person trapped in dualities. It is obvious that at each critical step in her life she could have made other choices, bringing the pursuit of *preyas* under the control of *śreyas* and done so altruistically rather than egoistically. She would then have awaited death, one presumes, with a sense of contentment—a cherished Hindu ideal[11]—and not in sorrow and repentance.

Appu is his mother's son in so far as he too is trapped in dualities—in the conflict between the 'desired' and the 'good' —though he appears to be firmer in his affirmation of the primacy of *śreyas* over *preyas*. It is in terms of this guiding principle of his life that he seeks to regulate his relations with his parents, Bhavaniammal and Indu. The eternal verities of human existence are symbolized for him by the Vedas, just as they are for his father and mother, but it seems that he would like to *live* by them while Dandapani and Alankaram only *use* them in their different ways. Appu's suffering arises not from a sense of sin (like Alankaram's) or failure (like Dandapani's) but from the moral effort required in subordinating nature to culture. Since he regards righteous conduct as binding on all, his parents' failure is his own failure too, and he suffers deeply for this reason too. There are, from this perspective, no individuals, no moral agents as such, but only relations which constitute the moral space.

The suffering which is the lot of Indu is of a different nature. She suffers from what seems to her to be the tyranny of *dharma*. She is married at a young age without her wishes being ascertained, for that is how Brahman girls get their husbands. She becomes a widow within three years and is expected to bear all the blame and burdens that widows do among Brahmans. If she does not bear the tell-tale mark of widowhood on her person—the shaven head—it is because her young husband specially made this request to Bhavaniammal when he had lost hope that he would live. Indu suffers for all this and more. She appeals to a higher *dharma*, that of 'conscience'. She seems to question the social or external basis of the moral life and

[11] See Chapter 5.

stresses 'sincerity' as the first moral principle. It is her sorrow that Appu does not understand her: they do not speak the same moral idiom. Her assertion that honesty such as hers (in acknowledging her love for Appu) is better than the deception Alankaram practises, and the 'external' adherence to morality which he himself seems to practise, leaves Appu speechless. His silence is not a heartless and mindless indifference, but born of sincere bewilderment—and this is the root of his suffering.

The moral struggles and agonies that are the stuff of life for Dandapani, Alankaram, Appu and Indu appear to have been overcome in Bhavaniammal's life. Not that she may not have suffered like the others; but, by the time we encounter her in the novel, she is sure of herself and has risen above such considerations as what other people may say about one's actions, such misfortunes as widowhood, and such virtues as a superficial reverence for the Vedas. Not for her the conflict between the 'desired' and the 'good', but her life is the very antithesis of Shivasu's, for she has endeavoured to absorb *preyas* into *śreyas*. Again, not for her the conflict between the culture and conscience—but then she is unlike both Indu and Alankaram. She is not like them because she seeks nothing for herself.

Bhavaniammal points to the possibility of attaining transcendence in human life through right choices, till a stage is reached when one is no longer in need of having to choose. Through her own life—by being what she is—she redeems others. She is the life-nurturing mother. While the nature of Alankaram's suffering 'provides the means by which death may be introduced or justified' (O'Flaherty 1976: 212), Bhavaniammal's sorrows, in contrast, have cleansed her own life and bestowed on her the capacity to bring peace and meaning into the lives of others. Her suffering may be said to have ripened her life to the point where it flowers into love and understanding. She has come as close to becoming like the Kaveri as any human being might. And this, indeed, is the human ideal—to reach beyond self and suffering, and to merge *preyas* and *śreyas* in a single vision of life.

5

LIVING AND DYING

Tell us that about which they doubt, O Death,
What there is in the great passing-on . . .

KATHA UPANISHAD

Alike for me is life and death:
Happy to live and happy to die,
I mourn for none, none mourns for me.

LAL DED

INTRODUCTORY

The attitudes of a people to death and dying should be viewed, it seems to me, in their totality, bringing out the inter-connectedness of belief, emotion and behaviour. This is not, however, what has been done generally by social anthropologists and sociologists writing on Hindu society. Beginning with Srinivas's classic study of the Coorgs (1952), through such detailed ethnographies of Indian villages as Berreman's (1963), down to such relatively recent monographs as those by Inden and Nicholas (1977) and Parry (1979), we have been provided more or less detailed analytical descriptions of mortuary rites and death pollution. But there has been very little (if any) discussion of the Hindu cognitive orientation to death. In this respect the 'field view' of death and dying seems to have turned out to be narrower than the 'book view'.[1] In fact, some recent innovative discussions of the theme have come from scholars whose work is based on textual analysis (see, for example, Malamoud 1975 and Das 1977). Parry (1982) is perhaps the first social anthropologist to have directed his inquiries in the

[1] Reflecting on the relative neglect of the study of death in its various aspects by sociologists specializing on Hindu society, it is amusing to recall what Rivers wrote well over half a century ago to one of his correspondents who was then working on a book on Kenyan tribes: 'Death is usually sufficiently important and rich in material to have a chapter to itself' (quoted in Langham 1981: 302).

field to this cognitive orientation, and he has obviously taken the texts seriously.

One way the sociologist might try to capture death as a 'total fact', which it is in the subjective experience of the bereaved, would be through the conceptualization of its cognitive, affective and behavioural aspects in terms of the notion of hierarchy. So viewed, the cognitive level (rather than aspect) is concerned with the significance of death in an encompassing cosmo-moral scheme of life. The behavioural level incorporates all the practical consequences of death, including the performance of rituals, formal mourning, affirmation or termination of social ties, division and inheritance of property, and so on. Finally, the affective level refers to the emotional impact of death on individuals, the personal grief and sorrow that they feel as a result of their bereavement. I would like to suggest that we will be able to provide much richer interpretations of behavioural and emotional responses to death—bringing out the structures of meaning and significance—if we consider first the cognitive orientations of the people concerned.

Such a holistic view places in proper perspective Hertz's profound observation that, since the 'physical individual' appears in society as a 'social being', his 'destruction' or death is a 'sacrilege' against society (Hertz 1960: 77). Taken by itself this observation and others in the same vein—for example, 'death . . . posits the most terrifying threat to the taken-for-granted realities of everyday life' (Berger and Luckmann 1967: 119)—may result in an overweening accent on the social significance of death at the cost of the personal or the subjective import. Our effort should be to connect them—the collective and personal perspectives—and consequently to make sense of living and dying as a single phenomenon or an integrated experience. Malinowski was quite right when he observed that 'he who is faced by death turns to the promise of life' (1948: 47) and this, needless to emphasize, is ultimately possible only cognitively.[2]

Having affirmed the importance of the cognitive level within

[2] According to Hindu tradition the rituals described in the *brāhmaṇa* texts had for their principal aim the extension of life and the overcoming of death. The promise of physical immortality held out in these texts has given way to the philosophical attitude of the Upanishads which emphasize overcoming death through

a holistic perspective on death, I would now like to focus on it as I have been able to understand it in the course of my studies of Kashmiri Pandit culture and society.[3] There are a number of studies dealing with the behavioural entailments following immediately after death, based on texts (for example, Pandey 1969) or observation (for example, Stevenson 1920), which are broadly true of the Pandits also. I will mention very briefly some post-mortuary rituals, since these bear upon my main argument. Any merit that the discussion might have would lie in providing a perspective for the study of the literature on rituals connected with death and the manes, inheritance rules, post-mortem social rearrangements, etc. Unfortunately, the study of bereavement in Hindu society from the point of view of subjective experience remains a relatively neglected area, but the data and analysis presented here also bear upon that aspect of death.

TYPES OF DEATH AND THEIR SIGNIFICANCE

Death in a Kashmiri village is naturally not an everyday occurrence, but its possibility is ever present and so is the concern with it. Moreover, its familiarity does not make it trivial. It is considered essentially a family event, though not all members of the family, or the narrower domestic group within it, are equally affected by it, whether emotionally, ritually or materially. Thus the death of an infant, or even a newly born baby, causes some emotional hurt to the mother, and perhaps the father, but hardly affects anybody else. This is understandable since the involvement of a growing child in social life is a gradual process, duly marked by the kind of 'rites of possage' van Gennep (1960) wrote about. By contrast, the death of a man in the prime of his youth is judged as being calamitous and has considerable ritual and material implications, not to speak of the emotional traumas it entails.

One often hears the Pandits exclaim '*marunai chu!*' (ah,

---

the termination of the cycle of birth, death and rebirth. The 'promise of life' is thus of more than one kind.

[3] See Madan 1965 and Chapter 1 above. I may add that there are many other points in this chapter which tie up with the discussion in Chapter 1 and it would involve too many cross-references to indicate all of them.

one has to die!) in the course of everyday conversation. I would like to suggest that this utterance does not so much refer to a fear of finitude, or accountability, which some philosophies of death dwell upon,[4] as to a concern with rectitude or morality in the conduct of everyday life. In the course of my discussions with the Pandits, I have often raised the question as to how one might know for sure that a particular person is morally upright, that he or she has led and continues to lead a 'good' life. Needless to emphasize, the word 'good' is not used here in any narrow sense of prudence or pragmatism but refers to moral imperatives as defined in Pandit culture. Not that worldly success is disdained: on the contrary, it is often argued by the Pandits that, if a man has done well by himself in a material or worldly sense—if he has health, wealth, sons and fame—then he has led a 'blessed' life, but that outward signs of this kind are not a true indication of his *indeed* having led a good life. The apparent success and good fortune that attends one in this, the present life (*ihaloka*) could well be the rich and deserved harvest of good actions (*karma*) in previous lives. Even while enjoying such good fortune, however, one may be sowing through bad deeds the seeds of suffering and sorrow for one's next life (*paraloka*).

Given such a moral calculus, how else does one know for certain that a person is leading a good life? The Pandits aver that there are some simple though not certain answers to this significant and complex question, besides the one mentioned above, namely, in terms of apparent worldly success. Thus, it is suggested that we should examine what a man is actually doing in his relations with other human beings and explore the spirit that motivates him. Does he look after his dependents well, particularly helpless widows and aged parents? Does he engage in prescribed ritual performances? Is he of a righteous (*dhārmika*) frame of mind? A person may be seen to be doing what is right and good, devoting himself and his material resources—body (*tana*) and wealth (*dhana*)—to leading a good life, but how do we know for certain that he is involved in doing so

[4] Kashmiri Muslims also use this expression ('one has to die!'), but in their case the notion of final reckoning on the day of judgement is present. The Pandits of course repudiate any such notion of final accountability, though not of retribution.

spiritually, applying his mind or spirit (*mana*) to it? There can be no spiritual involvement without sincerity. As the Pandits put it, the good life must not be merely led outwardly but, first of all, inwardly, 'by the truthful heart' (*pazidila*). But a person's sincerity—the inward condition—is difficult to fathom.

Is there, then, no way in which one can vouch for a person having led a good life? The Pandits maintain that the ultimate and critical sign of the good life may be available in the manner a person attains his death. I use the word 'attain' to emphasize that the ideal is to strive to die in a manner which underscores the active role of a person in his own death, as contrasted with the passivity conveyed by expressions like 'passing away' or 'dying'; even the phrase 'meet one's death' does not appear to be adequate. The point is not that the Pandits do not use words and expressions signifying simply the 'passing away' or 'passing beyond this life', for they do so, but that they emphasize the possibility of attaining a good death through letting go of, or renouncing, the life-breath (*prāṇatyāga*) voluntarily, in full command: as the Isha Upanishad says, may the life-breath enter into the immortal breath (17). It is, then, the good death that bears true witness to the good life.

The main elements of the notion of good death are the place (*sthāna*), the time (*kāla*), and the condition of the person (*pātra*) at the time of his death. The best place in which to die, according to the Pandits, is one's own home, the house in which one has lived. For most men this would also be the house where one was born,[5] but in the case of women it would be the house where one has lived after marriage and borne children. The house is not a mere dwelling but the microcosm of the universe (as discussed in Chapter 1 above). It is in the house that the householder (*gṛhastha*) pursues his legitimate worldly goals

[5] Pandit houses are made of fired brick, timber and mud-plaster or lime mortar. There are several houses in the villages I have visited which are more than a hundred years old. Every house is expected to last well beyond the life-span of its builders and the succeeding two generations. It is not surprising that people should develop a deep attachment to their homes. The idea that it is better to die away from home on the banks of a river, entertained by many Brahman communities, is not favoured by the Pandits, though they know about it as they do about the Rajput ideal of death on the battlefield.

(*dharma-karma*), and seeks to improve the moral quality of his person or self. It is, therefore, right and proper that he should die here. I will have more to say on this later.

The only preferred alternative is to die in a holy place such as Hardwar or Kashi. This is, however, seen as an appropriate end to the life of an unattached person—one who has no immediate kin or one who has overcome worldly attachments—rather than that of a householder. Some elderly Pandits (mostly men) do go to holy places during the winter, but this is seen more as a purificatory ritual—the washing-off of one's evil or sins—in preparation for the good death rather than the wish or hope to die at such a place.

So, one should die at home, but that is not enough to constitute a good death. One must die, besides, at an astrologically appropriate time, which would ensure a smooth transition from this world of human beings (*ihaloka*) to the worlds beyond, namely: the world of the death-god (*yamaloka*), where disembodied souls (*preta*) go after cremation until they attain the status of manes (*pitṛ*); the world of manes (*pitṛloka*); and, finally, back to this world or, best of all, to the world of gods (*svarga*), where one attains eternal bliss (*ānanda*) through the merger of the individual soul with the *Brahman* of which it is an emanation.[6]

Finally, there is the personal condition of the dying person: has he or she lived a long life marked by the fulfilment of legitimate worldly goals (*puruṣārtha*) of wealth, progeny (particularly sons), and fame among fellow human beings, as also by the pursuit of righteous conduct (*dharma*), the performance of rituals (*kriyā-karma*), and devotion (*bhakti*) to one's chosen deity (*iṣṭadeva* or *iṣṭadevī*)? Has death been attained peacefully and swiftly, in full command of one's physical and mental faculties? Do one's survivors include only those younger than

[6] There are two opinions prevalent among the Pandits regarding the precise nature of *svarga* (heaven) and *naraka* (hell). According to the one, these are places to which the disembodied person is taken after death and he spends as much time in each as is required by the calculus of retribution. Only thereafter is he reborn. According to the second, *svarga* and *naraka* are states of existence in this human world and the joys of the former and the tortures of the latter are experienced here itself. A disembodied person is reincarnated immediately after he makes the transition from the category of ghost to that of ancestor.

oneself, and, in the case of a woman, her husband, and are they well provided for?[7] More such elements in the personal condition of the dying person could be listed, but the most crucial of them all, I may repeat, is that one should die in full consciousness of the event, with one's mind fixed upon the Supreme God (*Bhagavān*) or the Divine Spirit (*Brahman*). Thus alone may one be sure that, even if one does not attain release (*mukti*) from reincarnation (*saṁsāra*), at least the next life will be better than that coming to its end. A person who departs thus, having fulfilled obligations, enjoyed the joys of the householder's life (*gārhasthya*), and 'chosen' the exact moment of his death, is said to have attained the 'good way of going' (*gat prāvin*; cf. the Sanskrit *sadgati* or *paramagati*, 'going the good or great way', and hence the Upanishadic poser quoted in the epigraph).

How many Pandits do, in fact, attain the good death as defined above? The answer to this question will have to be: very few. Quite understandably, therefore, the survivors always try to make claims, within the limits imposed by the actual circumstances of the death which has occurred, that some of the signs of the good death had, in fact, been present but that they had been unwise or blinded by excessive emotional attachment to the dying person not to take the cue and had, therefore, failed to understand what was being communicated to them. Some deaths—particularly of one's parents—are sought to be made into 'myths', not so much in some kind of perverse mendacity as in hopeful reaffirmation of some cardinal principles of the good life and in stressing that death, though painful, is not bad as such but that only a particular way of dying—denoting loss of self-control in life and in death—is so. In other words, what is said is true in the sense in which all myths are true, though it may not be a strictly factual description of the actual event. When the signs and indications that one looks for on such an occasion are more discernible than is common, grief and mourning among the survivors are mixed with thanksgiving. They may vie with one another in describing the last moments of the life of the departed person to visitors, kith and kin, who come to condole with them.

Good deaths, and the last words spoken by those who attain

[7] The Pandits say that the father who bequeaths debts to his sons is, in fact, a foe and not a friend: *ṛṇa kṛtā pitā śatruḥ*.

it, are remembered and talked about for edification for years. They constitute Pandit society's commentary on human life. Narayan Das died when he was more than ninety years old and was survived by sons and daughters, grandchildren and great-grandchildren. He had done well by himself as a businessman, acquired much property and built a big house. One of his sons was running successfully the business started by him, while another had acquired great fame in the Pandit community for his learning in Shaiva philosophy and for his saintly life. The old man's funeral was a celebration, complete with music, and the post-cremation community meals were indeed feasts.

Similarly, when Gangamal died, her aged husband escorted the dead body to the cremation ground. Her son, who was then in his mid-forties and held an important position as a civil servant, used to recall, years after her death, that many Pandit women had come out of their homes to pay obeisance to the dead body on its way to the cremation ground, exclaiming that they too hoped to die the same splendid way, that is, survived by an aged husband and a worthy son. Such a death becomes an auspicious event.

Now, this Pandit, an only son of his parents, had been deeply attached to his mother, and she had died a rather painful death. As the last moments of her life lingered on, the assembled kin and relatives had asked him to hold her feet in a gesture of pleading and ask her to give up her grip on life. The point about such advice is that the mother was believed to be clinging to life because she knew how grieved her son would be by her passing away. She had finally died with her son holding her feet and after he had expressed the wish for the end of the agony of her mortal frame.[8] In this case, a lingering and painful death was not interpreted to mean that the old lady had not led a good life: the blame was placed upon the excessive attachment of her son to her and only partly on her love for him. In any case, the mother–son bond is the very model for

[8] This seems to be a widely prevalent notion among Hindus. Thus, we read about the saint-mystic Ramakrishna, who, when suffering from painful throat cancer, whispered, '... I've gone on suffering like this because I am afraid you'll shed so many tears if I leave you. But if you will tell me, "That is enough suffering—let the body go", then I may give it up' (Isherwood 1965: 298).

virtuous human attachment. On his part, the son used to talk years later, till he himself died, of the special signs accompanying his mother's death to expound on her virtuous life.

A community which entertains a notion of the good death may be expected to complement it with a notion of the bad death. All the conditions and signs mentioned above are reversed to construct the paradigm of such a death. Thus, I was told of a priest who had died a bad death, after a protracted illness and there were no close kinsfolk to look after him. His wife had died before him and none of the sons born to them had survived into adulthood. His only surviving child was a daughter who, being married, was living with her own husband and children and, therefore, unable to attend on him on a full-time basis. His lingering death in rather sordid surroundings was attributed by some informants to the stealthy involvement of the deceased in *pretakriyā*, that is, the rituals of invoking ghosts to assist in human affairs, for good or for bad. He was a priest-sorcerer. It was recalled that when he walked about after nightfall dogs invariably barked at him.

A bad death is more often explained in terms of the burden of the bad *karma* of the previous birth. There was the case of an old man paralysed for three years, unable to move a leg and arm, unable to eat properly, speechless, but with an alert mind and eyes that could see and ears that could hear. Among those looking after him were a daughter, who had become a widow within days of her marriage at the age of sixteen, and a son who was a simpleton. To have such a daughter and also such a son living under one's roof is the worst misfortune that may befall a Pandit. The old man himself had been known to be a good man; the tortures he suffered as a father and his tragic last years were, therefore, seen by the people around him as the bitter fruit of bad *karma* in his previous life. A bad death certifies the existence of the cosmo-moral order just as the good death does. The question that may be raised at this point is whether death in certain circumstances points to moral chaos, the breakdown of the *nomos*.

Now, the Pandits do indeed entertain the notion of what may be called 'anomic' death, that is, death which raises misgivings, even if only temporarily, regarding the fragility of the moral foundations of human life. When these foundations seem to be vulnerable to death, then death does, indeed, appear as a terrifying 'onslaught of the nightmare' (Berger and Luckman 1967: 119). The death of an old couple's youthful son, married and with dependent children, is the prime example of what the Pandits call 'untimely or premature death', but this literal translation of the phrase *akāla mṛtyu* hardly captures the intensity of moral horror and personal sorrow which are sought to be conveyed when they use it. They also refer to such an event as *pralaya*, or the dissolution of the cosmo-moral order, for it upsets the natural–moral ordering of events—hence my characterization of it as anomic death. While the aged parent or parents lose the moral and perhaps the material mainstay of their old age, the young wife is stigmatized and even feared for the rest of her life and excluded from active participation in auspicious ceremonies. As for the children, orphans arouse as much sympathy in Pandit society as anywhere else. Ultimately such a death is also made bearable by invoking the notion of *karma:* even the unbearable is never *really* undeserved.

The notion of *pralaya* is also invoked sometimes to interpret collective deaths. However, such cases are rare, being confined to road accidents and very occasionally drowning and house-fires. Malefic spirits are sometimes held responsible for such occurrences, but more typically they are considered mysterious instances of the convergence of individual karmic trajectories, and, therefore, extremely inauspicious. In 1957, when I first arrived in the village of Utrassu-Umanagri for fieldwork, the villagers still had fairly fresh memories of what they had heard about the widespread killings of Pandits in the north-western parts of the Kashmir valley which had been raided by thousands of tribesmen from Pakistan ten years earlier. They had also heard or read about the communal riots in Panjab and Bengal in 1946–7. The older villagers remembered the Bihar and Quetta earthquakes of the mid-1930s. The consensus about these brutal events was, firstly, that the death of the victims had been ordained in this very manner—the notion of the convergence of individual karmic destinies in a collective catastrophe—and, secondly, that such events are indicative of a general decline of *dharma*: they are a foretaste, as it were, of the ultimate dissolution (*pralaya*) of the present degenerate age, the *kaliyuga*.

There is yet another kind of death recognized by the Pandits which should be mentioned here. In 1957 Tarachand Pandit was one of the older men (then in his mid-sixties) of Utrassu-Umanagri. He belonged to an 'aristocratic' family and was much respected for his knowledge of traditional sacred lore. He was well-versed in Sanskrit and also known for his upright personal life. When he died a couple of years later, I was informed of the event by letter by a couple of informants who regretted his passing away as it marked the end of the days of learned men endowed with traditional knowledge. I believe what these informants were trying to convey to me was that the old man had been an exemplar of the social–moral order and piety; therefore, his life had been exceptionally meaningful, inasmuch as it illumined the meaningfulness of life for members of his community: it offered them guidelines for action. His death grievously deprived the community of these guidelines, of the knowledge of moral precepts and rules for social action. It too was, I would like to suggest, a case of the threat of anomie of an exceptional kind. This fear of a decline into normlessness, or into a society whose norms might be strange or even abhorrent, was not felt by all the Pandits of the village, nor in the same measure by those who apprehended it. In any case (and as pointed out above) the Pandits always talk of the increasing moral degeneration of the *kaliyuga*. For those among them who seriously entertain the notion of moral degeneration from *satyayuga* (the age of truth) to *kaliyuga* (the age of ignorance and untruth), the death of Tarachand had a deep though not unexpected significance.

I should like to point out here that many deaths entail certain practical consequences and necessitate some social re-arrangements, but it would be erroneous to consider them anomic for that reason. Let me illustrate by mentioning the cases of Somavati and Prabhavati, two widows of the village of Utrassu-Umanagri. In 1957 they were both in their early thirties. When they were widowed, each had an infant son. Though the terrible blow of widowhood abolishes all distinctions between one Pandit woman and another, it was apparent that with the passage of time the sympathy of the villagers had come to lie more with Prabhavati than Somavati. The latter belonged to a very prosperous land-owning household and everybody knew that she and her infant son had not suffered from want. She was the only adult literate woman of the village and was generally recognized as an intelligent person who had been able to manage her affairs quite well.

In contrast, Prabhavati belonged to a poor household with only a small land-holding. She was considered to be a simple woman, even simple-witted, and at the mercy of her deceased husband's elder brother (and his family) who was regarded as being a very selfish person. Many instances of his selfishness were cited and, in this context, the fact of his being a very prosperous person was underscored. Once, when I asked Prabhavati's son (then aged seventeen) what his feelings about his deceased father were, his reply was: 'Curse the fellow! I don't even have a memory of him.'

These two cases bring out how two deaths, which have the same ritual significance, and may be expected to have similar emotional significance, are yet very different in terms of the practical consequences they have: so much so, indeed, that even the emotional reactions acquire a hue other than what may be normally expected, as is evident from Prabhavati's son's total indifference to his deceased father. Normally, the Pandits readily resort to paeans when talking of their fathers as a matter of conventional morality, if not of personal sentiment.

The rearrangement of social relations that follows a death may also have variable significance. While widows may live on sufferance or may be looked after well (the latter is usual), widowers remarry if they can manage it (which is not always easy because of a shortage of women). Remarriage may create conflict along an expected though regrettable course of events. Ratanlal's mother died when he was about ten years old. His father, though in his late forties, married a young woman who soon bore him a daughter. The villagers maintained that Ratanlal's father was totally infatuated with his second wife who had no maternal feelings for the boy and contributed to the emergence of an emotional distance between father and son. The death of a mother is grievous enough, but the arrival of a stepmother, particularly if the paternal grandparents are dead, may amount to, in the words of an informant, 'an invisible second death'—that is, as far as the child is concerned, for he loses not only his mother (by death) but also his father (by estrangement). In the normal course of events, the inauspiciousness of a death in the family is finally and best removed by the auspiciousness of marriage and childbirth,[9] but the practical consequences of a particular marriage may dictate a negative evaluation of it, as in the foregoing case.

While we are dealing with the consequences of widowers remarrying, it is pertinent to mention the Pandit attitude to a wife's death. Widowers suffer from none of the ritual or social disabilities that widows do. When a widower seeks to remarry (or his elders desire him to do so), the tallying of horoscopes, which is a prerequisite of any marriage and is undertaken by the girl's family, will be carried out with great care. A potential 'wife killer' (in the sense that his horoscope contains a *yoga*, or conjunction of astral bodies called *graha*, which will result in his wife's death) makes a good match for a potential 'husband killer'. On the whole, 'husband killers' are more feared than 'wife killers' and a man who has lost two wives may yet be able to marry a third time, though he may secretly pay a bride price (see Madan 1965: 118).

The point I want to stress here is that, apart from the very limited ritual and social consequences of widowerhood, a man is expected to keep his emotional feelings on the death of his wife entirely to himself and give no public expression to his grief. A man grieving openly over his wife's death only invites ridicule, not sympathy. There is the case of Damodar, whose wife died when he was in his sixties and both his sons were living with him in the same household along with their wives and children. For a Pandit in this kind of situation, the death of his wife is expected to be hardly an occasion for grieving. But Damodar did grieve, chiding his sons and daughters-in-law for being happy in their conjugal bliss, while his own wife had, as he put it, deserted him. The reaction of his children and all those who learnt about his behaviour was one of disbelief and ridicule.

While some deaths are regarded as having a manifold significance, others may be considered non-events or even welcomed. Still-births, or the death of a baby before it has cut teeth, are

[9] See Chapter 2 above.

non-events in ritual and social terms. That the mother may suffer emotionally by such a death is another matter. As Hertz (1960) clearly pointed out, the death of a child may arouse no emotion, occasion no ritual, and go unnoticed since such collective responses are linked to the social status of the deceased. In these respects a child is indeed like a stranger. Moreover, the death of badly malformed babies is welcomed, not so much out of pity for the baby itself as out of fear that it may be ominous. The mother of such a child is also looked upon with suspicion as the original source of ill luck. It is difficult to tell how often such babies are born: I was told of only one instance and, apart from a blind boy, there were no Pandits in Utrassu-Umanagri who suffered from a serious physical handicap. Also, it should be stated here, I did not even hear any rumours of infanticide.

Killing of any kind, whether of children or adults, of one's own self (*ātmahatyā*) or of others (*manuṣyahatyā*), is totally disapproved of in Pandit culture.[10] It is argued that since no individual is really responsible for his own or another's birth—this being the result of *karma* or of divine blessing—he has no moral right to end his own life or kill others. Suicide is a secretive act of self-punishment, giving expression to a sense of frustration, guilt or dishonour. But, the Pandits maintain, suicide transfers the individual's sense of dishonour to the family and may, therefore, never be regarded as an act of self-sacrifice, which must be oriented towards others.

Killing another Pandit is a heinous sin, for it involves taking the life of a Brahman (*brahmahatyā*) which is equivalent to the killing of a cow (*gauhatyā*) in the scales of evil. There is an allotted life-span for each individual (calculable from the horoscope) and the end will come at the appointed time and in a

[10] Though a distinction would be made between dying by fasting or by some violent means, suicide is clearly condemned. This attitude is not shared by all other Brahman and non-Brahman communities. Thus, there is the tradition of *prāyopaveśan*, or fasting to death, in Maharashtra, and the most recent example of this which attracted national attention was the passing away in 1982 of Vinoba Bhave, after he had decided to abstain from all nourishment and medication following a heart attack. He was 88. The practice of fasting to death is, of course, positively affirmed among Jaina laymen (see Jaini 1979: 181). The Jaina influence among many Hindu communities, particularly in western India, is well known.

manner that may or may not appear just but always has its hidden justification. To try to interfere with this process is to incur sin of a magnitude which would wash away the merit of all the good deeds of a lifetime. There was no known case of suicide or homicide among the Pandits of Utrassu-Umanagri, but I was given details of two cases of suicide by poisoning from elsewhere. My informants did, however, maintain that should an unmarried girl or widow become pregnant she may commit suicide or may be poisoned by her parents. But even in such circumstances the moral wrongdoing of the girl concerned would perhaps be less heinous than the sinful act of her suicide or of killing her.

To conclude this description of types of death, I should mention the death of a holy man, an adept in *yoga*, a renouncer, or one whom the Pandits call an *ātmajñānī*, that is, a person who has achieved a realization of his true nature as inseparable from the Supreme Spirit (*Brahman*). There are not many people of this kind to be found in Kashmir, but I was given accounts of some such deaths by several informants. In fact, such a person is not said to have died but attained *mukti* (release from the physical body) or *samādhi*, the state of non-dualistic union with the *Brahman*, in which the passage of time (*kāla*) loses all meaning and death (Kala) holds no fears. Besides, such a person does not join the category of manes and his post-mortuary rituals are different from those of ordinary householders.

The entry of a person into *samādhi* is a very solemn occasion, for he is considered to have transcended birth and death, and calls for the paying of homage rather than the expression of personal grief, which is nevertheless experienced by those who were closely associated with the deceased. 'They grieve', an informant told me, 'because they fail to understand their guru's teaching, though they may have served him well. The true disciple will not grieve, for life and death are of no significance compared to the craving of the individual soul to achieve union with the *Brahman*.' A Kashmiri hymn says:

> I have wandered through the grooves of conception,
> Experienced childhood, youth and old age repeatedly;
> In many garbs have I played the actor (clown):
> Take me now unto yourself and free me from the
> bondage of duality.

The refrain of the hymn is the exhortation: 'End your isolation, O lonely one (*kevala*) through union with the unique (*kaivalya*).'

Having characterized deaths as good, bad or anomic, as expected, untimely or welcome, it is of some interest to note here that the Pandits also entertain the notion of what may be called the 'averted' death, that is a death that may have occurred but did not. The most common example is of people who recover from a very critical illness after hope of survival has been given up. The non-occurrence of death in such cases is attributed to the notion that the allotted life-span had not yet been completed. Also, divine grace (*anugraha*) is invariably mentioned as the saviour of human beings in all situations of distress and danger.

A person's death may be anticipated on the basis of astrological calculation when he is reckoned to be under the influence of a conjunction of *graha* indicative of a 'second birth' (*dvi-janama yoga*). The danger to life is judged to be acute but the hope of survival (a second birth, as it were) is also entertained. Rituals of various kinds are performed to avert death, the most notable of these being *tulābhār*, that is, the weighing of the body against grain and giving away the grain to a priest or some other person willing to receive it. The body of the threatened person is thus symbolically discarded and replaced through an act of transfer or exchange.

A third example of averted death is rather rare and involves cases where a person is believed to have actually died and come back to life. I met one such person, a man in his sixties, who told me of his 'death' following an illness. He found himself in a state of dreaming (*svapna avasthā*) and taken away by the messengers of death, who appeared to him as two beautiful women, to the abode of the dead (*yamaloka*). There they were told by some 'functionary', after he had consulted a 'red-covered register', that they had got the wrong man. He soon awoke and found his family members wailing over his 'death'. His death had finally been averted, he said, because his time to 'go' had not yet arrived. Such incidents are referred to as cases of 'mistaken identity' (*nāv badlī*, 'change of name').

I may mention one more and a different type of case in

illustration of the notion of averted death. The first wife of Sudama, one of the old men of Utrassu-Umanagri, had borne him eleven children but they had all died in infancy. She too had then died. Sudama married again (at the age of forty-one) and his second wife began her motherhood by losing her first-born child. A few years later she gave birth to a second child, a boy, who was sixteen years old in 1957, and who had been appropriately named Lassa ('may you live!'). He had overcome what Sudama considered his own bad luck, the result of the wrong doings of his previous life or lives. The fact that his second wife bore him no more children, though she was only twenty-three years old at the time of Lassa's birth, was seen by Sudama as evidence of his bad luck. He told me that the survival of Lassa after the death of twelve children was the result of the blessings of the many saintly men whom he and his wife had visited and, ultimately, of divine grace. Lassa too might well have died (or not been born at all) but his death had been averted.

The foregoing discussion of Pandit ideas about death and dying, though presented here piecemeal as a taxonomy, is derived from their discourse on these important themes, and this discourse springs from a unified consciousness. It also guides behavioural responses to death. I will now describe some of these responses.

THE DAY OF DEATH AND AFTER

Whatever the circumstances of a particular death of an adult (that is, a ritually intiated person rather than a person of a certain age), certain actions have to be performed following it which throw further light on the Pandit attitude to dying. The last moments of a Pandit's life are accompanied as long as possible by a reading of the Bhagavad Gita, particularly the verses (in chapter II) describing the imperishability of the soul. If time and other circumstances allow, the dying person may make the gift of a cow (*gopradāna*) to a priest: the decision to do so may not be his or her own, but that of the family. This absolves one of all the moral lapses that may have occurred during one's lifetime. In place of a cow an image of the animal cut out in gold, silver, or copper (obtained in advance, perhaps by the person himself) may be given away. If water from the river Ganga is available (in one's own home or with some other family in the village), a few drops are poured into the mouth of the dying person. If Ganga water is not available, water in which a *sālagrāma* (the black stone representation of Vishnu) has been washed may be used. The purpose of such administration of holy water is to relieve the dying person of moral imperfections and to cleanse his or her body of physical impurities.

As soon as death occurs, the event which is essentially domestic, and in that sense private and indoor, is made public through loud weeping and wailing by women and children. Men may shed tears but they are expected not to wail. Weeping by women occurs in other domestic situations also, but the stylized wailing associated with death is very distinctive and announces a death to the neighbourhood. Intense activity is thus generated: neighbours (kith and kin) rush in, messengers rush out to carry the news to all concerned and to perform other chores, the family priest arrives (or some other priest who may substitute for him in his absence), and preparations for the last life-cycle ritual begin. In short, it is a situation of much emotional stress, much movement and much talk. Wailing includes talk addressed to the dead person, to the survivors, or to oneself, recalling events, expressing grief and perhaps helplessness, and so on. The visitors who assemble offer consolation and try to control the mourners who tear their clothes and hair and slap and scratch their faces. They also make arrangements for the cremation and the feeding of the family, for no food will be cooked for three to twelve days by the first of kin of the deceased. Not only are the close kin in mourning, they are also in a state of pollution and food cooked by them would be unacceptable to more distant kin and relatives who are present in the house or arrive there. The latter suffer from pollution of a shorter duration or none at all.

Soon the rituals begin, marked by the priests' recitations in Sanskrit. The body is removed from amidst the mourners for ritual bathing and other rites. I will not go into the details of these rites but only mention their special character. Cremation is called the 'ritual of burning' (*dāhasaṁskāra*) and is the culmination of the 'last ritual' (*antim saṁskāra*). As such, it marks the closure of the series of rituals concerning the human body, which begin with the rite for conception, and mark the step-by-step process of maturation. One's moral maturation is thus complete only when the body is cremated: in fact, cremation offers the opportunity for release from transmigration if one has reached a state of perfection—a most rare happening. The cremation, like all fire offerings, is intended to carry upwards (to the gods) that which is entrusted to Agni, the fire god. However, all post-cremation rites are of a distinctive character, being *pitṛkriyā* (rites for ancestors) and not *devakriyā* (rites for gods).[11]

After cremation, the disembodied dead person remains in the transitional condition of *preta* (ghost) for eleven days, during which time various rites are performed and food offerings made to sustain the *preta* as also placate it, for it is dangerous. The rituals on the eleventh day signal the entry or transformation of the *preta* into the category of *pitṛ* (manes). Thereafter, offerings of food (*śrāddha*) are normally made to them biannually—on the death anniversary and during the 'fortnight of manes' (*kāmbarpacha*) in autumn, and of water (*treś*, *tarpaṇa*) every morning as an act of piety (*śraddhā*). 'As we do for our ancestors so will our sons and grandsons do for us': this was said to me repeatedly, stressing the continuity of the lineage and, I might add, producing a meaningful symbolic universe comprising the *sapiṇḍa* (see Dumont 1982).

[11] I should here mention my inability at present to state explicitly the Pandit position in respect of the assertion made by a number of scholars in recent years that cremation is a sacrificial act (see, for example, Das 1977; Parry 1981 and 1982). I have never heard any Pandit refer to cremation by any word other than *dāhasaṁskāra* and the words used for fire sacrifice (*havan*) or animal sacrifice (*balī*) are not used. Nor have I heard the dead body referred to as *āhuti*, that which is offered in a fire sacrifice. But I have not had the opportunity to check all this thoroughly. Parry introduces a further complexity in the situation by maintaining that 'the householder sacrifices himself on his funeral pyre in order that he may be reborn' (1982: 74). I am quite sure that the Pandits consider the son of the deceased parent as the 'performer' who earns merit by performing the last rites. They quote the various *smṛtis* and Puranas on this point. Moreover, the prime concern in the proper performance of mortuary rites is to ensure the safe passage of the *preta* (disembodied spirit) into the category of *pitṛ* (manes). The manes are related to their descendants in a reciprocal relationship of dependence: without receiving food offerings they go to hell, but then their erring descendants also are accursed.

The post-cremation situation is complex for at least two reasons. Firstly, not all who die enjoy the same status as manes: for example a young man who dies before becoming a parent is not comparable to a married man survived by sons. Also, there is quite some ambiguity regarding what happens after the disembodied *preta* becomes the *pitṛ*. It would seem that in some symbolic sense, as an 'image' (*ākarā*), the *pitṛ* remains in the 'land' of the manes but is at the same time reincarnated here on the earth. Thus, in the relationship between the living and the dead, the notions of *pitṛ* (ancestor) and *punarjanma* (rebirth) negate the notion of death as a terminal event. It is an event of critical importance in the worldly life of an individual but of no consequence for his 'inner self' or soul (*ātmā*). A good life vouched by a good death does, however, take one a step further on the very long journey to freedom from the chain of birth–death–rebirth. To be worthy of grace (*anugraha*) would seem to be what the Pandits hope for in this quest for *mukti*. One of the most commonly recited Sanskrit prayers of the Pandits (which appears to be a *mélange* drawn from various sources) says: 'Born again, to die again, and then be conceived again . . . fearful of terrifying hells, I tremble with fear, O lord of the lowly, take me across unto Yourself'.[12]

Death is, then, made bearable in Pandit culture by its being treated as an opportunity for the individual soul to realize union with 'that' from which it has got separated—the *kaivalya-kevala* reunion of the Kashmiri didactic song I quoted earlier, in both of which one hears reverberations of the Upanishads. The Pandits' preoccupation with this reunion is but an echo of the Kaivalya Upanishad's repeated exhortation, '*kaivalyam padam aśnute, kaivalyam padam aśnute*', that is, 'he merges with the unique, with the unique he merges'. Similarly, the Katha Upanishad says: 'If one fails to attain Brahman before one's body falls away, one must then don a body again to return to the world of created things' (II.3.4); but 'the knowing self is never born and it never dies' (I.2.18).

It is not only through rituals and metaphysics that the Pandits

[12] *Punarapi jananam punarapi maranam punarapi garbhanivāsam/*
ghoram hara mama narakaripo keśava kalmaṣa bhāram/
māmanukampaya dinamanātham kuru bhavasāgara pāram.

attempt to cope with death but also through mythology. After a death has occurred, particularly of a parent, a learned priest is invited to read to the bereaved from the Garuda Purana, or some other suitable text, with a view to dilating upon the ephemeral nature of human life and thereby helping them to overcome their grief. The telling of such stories (*kathā*) in a formal manner is a mediating link between the abnormal speech forms that are triggered, as it were, by death, such as wailing (*vilāpa*) or withdrawal into silence (*dam-phuti*), and normal everyday speech forms.

Besides the strength derived from Puranic tales, an awareness of myths of various kinds, which is not unusual in a traditional Brahman community, also helps place life and death in a proper perspective. Let me illustrate this point. For the Pandits the family is indistinguishable from the house, which, as stated earlier, is not treated as a mere dwelling of economic value but also carries considerable emotional and cultural significance (see Madan 1965: 45–55). The same word *gara* (or *ghara*) is used to refer to both the family and the house and the latter is seen as symbolizing the cosmo-moral order. When the foundations of a new house are laid, rituals are performed to invoke the blessings of gods (notably Ganesha, the god who bestows auspiciousness and success on human actions) and to appease malevolent spirits. Among the benevolent deities invoked are the *kśetrapāla,* the guardians of the domain (space). When the construction of the house is completed, two small clay (or brass) pots are ceremonially installed in the kitchen which is a demarcated sacred space of critical importance in the Pandit home. These pots are brought in from the earlier house in which the family lived and are significantly called the *sanivāri,* 'the eternal pots', that is, the pots symbolizing perpetuity. Then the fire is lit ceremonially for the first time in the kitchen hearth and the primeval fire-god Agni thereby installed in the house. If the family have had any sacred icons (such as a *liṅgam*, a *śālagrāma*, and *śriyantra* symbolizing Shiva, Vishnu and Devi respectively) these too are ritually installed in the central room above the ground floor which is called the *ṭhokur-kuṭh*, 'the gods' room'. Besides the hearth, every traditional house has a fire altar for the performance of fire rituals (*homa*). Each house is also believed to have its own protective deity called the *gharadevatā* (the god of the house) and is identified with the Vedic god Vastoshpati at the time of the early winter feast in his honour.

Vastoshpati is the god of the dwelling place (*vāstu*) and he is also the protector of the sacred or moral order, for he is the enforcer of divine law (*vratapā*). It is thus through the connection with this god that a Pandit house becomes the microcosm of the universe and the members of the family represent humanity. It may be recalled here that the Rig Veda (I.71) tells us that Vastoshpati himself arose from the seed spilled by the Divine Father when his sexual intercourse with his daughter Ushas (Dawn) was interrupted by Agni, who shot an arrow at him for committing violence against the undifferentiated whole, the 'uncreated'. But Agni also warmed (cooked) the spilled seed into progeny, that is, into differentiated creation.

Agni is thus a central figure in this myth of genesis as told to me by some informants. And Agni finds a place in the Pandit hearth where food (a handful of rice) is offered to him before cooking starts in the morning. He thus sustains life. Ritual offerings (*homa*) are made to Agni periodically (some families do this fortnightly, *pakśāga*) and he serves as the mediator between the family and the gods. The important life-cycle rituals of initiation (*mekhalā*) and marriage (*nethar*) are also performed in front of Agni, as is the biannual rite of feeding the manes (*śrāddha*). Finally, it is to Agni that the dead body of a Pandit is entrusted, though this is done at a cremation site (*śmaśān*) and not at home. The home where daily rituals, births, initiations, marriages and rituals for ancestors take place is conceptually the very opposite of the cremation site for the burning of dead bodies, but these places and these critical events of family life are united through Agni, who emerges as a mediator between gods and men, the cosmos and earthly dwelling, this world (*ihaloka*) and the next (*paraloka*).

The manner in which the Pandits conceptualize death and dying is discernible in the post-mortuary rituals they perform, in their metaphysical traditions, and in the mythology which is always present in their minds as memory and is recalled in the didactic stories (*kathā*) which are told and listened to from time to time. What appears to be critical to their attitude is that death is not associated with finitude, though the inevitability of death is acknowledged and, in fact, greatly emphasized. Moreover, death is not seen as a threat to or a sacrilege against the social order. The cultural ideology of the Pandits stresses the importance of placing death in its proper context, which is provided first by the imperishability of the soul and then by the perishable nature of the body (*śarīra*) which is referred to *kṣṇabhaṅgur*, 'that which may dissolve any moment'. While the learned and the wise may conclude from such ideas that grieving over death is the result of ignorance and wordly attachments (*māyājāl*), common people do nevertheless grieve and express sorrow over death, and often see in it the need for certain social rearrangements, as, for example, when a young, childless widow returns to live in her natal home from where she had been 'carried away' (*vivāha*) as a bride.

In the foregoing discussion I have focused on the Pandits' cognitive orientation to dying and death and tried to show how it provides the cultural setting for an interpretation of what people do and what they think and perhaps feel in the event of a death. In other words, it is because death causes both a rent in the social fabric (as Hertz would have it) and a personal bereavement that the importance of the cognitive stance that the wise do not sorrow over death should be stressed. And the wise are the exemplars of proper conduct. The Pandit eschatology does not say that death is an insignificant event but that it is important enough for one to prepare for it; yet it is only an event in a chain to be followed by other events (births and deaths), just as it has been preceded by similar events. In the words of an informant, 'Only the unwise try to find the last bead in a rosary or the starting point on the potter's wheel.'

The roots of Pandit eschatology lie in ancient Brahmanical traditions. I have already indicated the Upanishadic reverberations in it, as also its explicit reliance upon Puranic mythology. The epics, particularly the Ramacharitmanas of Tulsidasa, with its deep devotional fervour, are also cited to expound the style and content of the good life. It is important to note, however, that what we are dealing with here is in fact an oral tradition, for though almost all Pandit men in rural Kashmir are literate, only a small minority among them are proficient in Sanskrit or know the texts well. Many of my informants are hardly aware of the precise textual sources of the elements of their beliefs. Their cultural tradition in respect of the goals of life and their eschatology, however, belong beyond any doubt to the family of Brahmanical traditions, and it is this, among other things, that I have tried to bring out in this chapter.

The Pandit world-view reflects the classical Indian doctrine of *karma* tempered by the later devotional Shaivism and Vaishnavism. Such a synthesis of early and medieval religious traditions is, of course, found in the lives of Hindus everywhere. 'One is born, and one has to die', said one of my informants, 'but one must not forget one's proper conduct (*dharma-karma*) in between, nor forget God either, for one should know that though trivial in themselves, these events "enclose" a great opportunity to improve one's moral fibre and move forward slowly towards ultimate release from the grip of life and death.' In sum, it is not birth or death, or the living and the dead, or gods and human beings, that matter, but the efforts to establish the proper relations between them. And that is what *bhaṭṭil*, the Pandit way of life, is all about.

EPILOGUE

THE QUEST FOR HINDUISM

There is no Hindu conception answering to the term 'Hinduism', and the question . . . 'What is Hinduism?' can only be answered by defining what it is that the foreigners who use the word mean by the term.

BANKIMCHANDRA CHATTERJI

One and indivisible at the root, it has grown into a vast tree with innumerable branches. The changes in the seasons affect it. It has its autumn and summer, its winter and spring. The rains nourish and fructify it too. Hinduism is like the Ganges, pure and unsullied at its source, but taking in its course the impurities in the way.

MAHATMA GANDHI

ANDRÉ MALRAUX: Life estranged from religion seems to me roughly contemporaneous with the machine age. . . . The new factor could be summed up as . . . the intoxication which enables action to ignore the legitimization of life . . .

JAWAHARLAL NEHRU: For how long?

INTRODUCTORY

If our quest for Hinduism in the modern world should take us to a home of the people called Hindus, or to one of their temples, we would be unlikely to find it there. We may receive some intimations of it in an Indian university; but it is in places such as the British Museum that we are sure to encounter it. I say so because the Hindus have not been particularly self-conscious about their religion as an isolable aspect of their world-view or of their way of life.[1] It is outsiders, non-Indians,

[1] See, for example, the following categorical statement by Bankimchandra Chatterji, one of the tallest Indians of the nineteenth century: 'With other peoples, religion is only a part of life; there are things religious and things lay and secular. To the Hindu, his whole life was religion. . . . To the Hindu, his relations to God and his relations to man, his spiritual life and his temporal life, are incapable of

who have felt the need to give a name to these people and characterize their religion. In one of the ancient Hindu texts, the Vishnu Purana, they are described as 'Bhāratī', that is, the children of the land called Bhārat, which is itself defined geographically, as the country lying north of the ocean and south of the snow-clad mountains.[2]

The Persians and Greeks, too, characterized these people in terms of the westernmost of the many great rivers of their land, the river called Sindhu in Sanskrit, Hindu in Persian and Indos in Greek. Later, in the eighth century, the Arabs transformed Sindhu into al-Hind, and used the word to refer to the people of the country, which its Muslim rulers still later called Hindustan, or the land of the Hindus. But the name Hindu did not have a simple geographical referent: it became a value-loaded term of reference for those Indians who had not yet been converted to Islam. One of the finest and most detailed books about the philosophy, sciences, customs and attitudes of Hindus was written by an eleventh-century visiting Muslim scholar, Abu Raihan Muhammad al-Biruni. It came to be called *Kitab-ul-Hind*, the book of India.

Similar books were to be written later by more distant visitors, namely, Western Christian missionaries, Western scholars, and imperial administrators. It was they who coined the term 'Hinduism' and its other European equivalents, such as Hinduismus, hindouisme and induismo, and wrote or spoke of the religion of the Hindus. One of the most perceptive of these commentators, Max Weber, noting that only recently had 'the Indians themselves begun to designate their religious affiliation as Hinduism', cautioned against reading into this usage meanings associated with the word religion in the West (see Weber 1958: 4). When an Indian has to use an Indian-language equivalent for Hinduism, the by now well established

---

being so distinguished. They form one compact and harmonious whole, to separate which into component parts is to break the entire fabric. All life to him was religion and religion never received a name from him, because it never had for him an existence apart from all that had received a name' (quoted in Chaudhuri 1979: 11–12). This finds echoes in the writings of many twentieth-century Hindu intellectuals, a recent example being Nirad Chaudhuri (1979).

[2] *Uttaram yat samudrasya / himādreścaiva dakṣiṇam, / varśam tad Bhāratam nāma / Bhāratī yatra santatiḥ.* Vishnu Purana III, 3.1.

choice is *hindū dharma* or *sanātana dharma*, meaning the Hindu norms of life or the eternal and universal norms of life. It should be pointed out that a mere way of life is not meant but, explicitly, a way of life lived in the light of norms. '*Dharma* is, then, the "form" of things as they are and the power that keeps them as they are and not otherwise' (Zaehner 1962: 3).

It is thus clear that the concept of *dharma* refers to what people do and to the beliefs that urge them to do what they do in a particular manner. Both 'purposes' and 'procedures' are laid down, encompassing the entire range of human situations and activities appropriate to them. The distinction between the 'religious' and the 'secular', which is fundamental in Western thought, is not easily made here. Such a differentiation, and further elaborations of it (most notably, the sacred–profane dichotomy), are a characteristic of the outsider's effort to understand Hindu society and have also entered the consciousness of the 'modern' Indian, who is by definition an alienated person. The autonomy of the domain of religion in Hindu society is postulated from outside: it represents at best legitimate anthropological procedure, but, if one is not careful, may result in a thoughtless and injurious fragmentation of the integrality of actual experience.

Contrary to what may be assumed, the Indian villager has even today a far more comprehensive and, therefore, complex view of the wholeness of life, though the manner in which he goes about the business of living hardly betrays any strains arising out of this complexity. The Hindu world-view when examined anthropologically—that is, from the outside but in the light of the principles that the people themselves enunciate (see Dumont 1970: 7)—is permeated by the notions of the divine and the sacred. This would seem to be not only the significance of, but also the warrant for Louis Dumont's exhortation that, in dealing with aspects of 'change' in contemporary India, the starting point should be the recognition of religion as constitutive of human society (ibid.: 94). The process of change will then be seen as being, among others, the process of the redefinition of the relationship of religion and society. All traditional societies today, and Indian society among them, are as much in quest of this redefinition as they are of development or modernization: in fact, the latter entails the former.

THE HINDU ENCOUNTER WITH CHRISTIANITY AND THE WEST

In view of the foregoing remarks, it is imperative that we begin by going back to the impact of the West on India, for the contemporary ideals of secularism and economic development have arisen from it, though this combination of goals was not what the contact first intimated to Indians. The struggle for the European control of India began with the coming of traders, followed by the arrival of Roman Catholic missionaries in Goa on the western coast of India early in the sixteenth century. After some inept efforts by Franciscan and Dominican friars, it was really the Jesuits who established Christianity with some of its cultural accoutrements, first in south India, and then in the north, where their task was made relatively easy by the religious tolerance and syncretism advocated and practised by the great Mughal emperor Akbar during the sixteenth century.

Roberto de Nobili came to the ancient and holy city of Madurai in 1606. He learned Sanskrit, the language of the sacred texts of Hinduism—old-time Hindus used to call it the language of the gods—and studied them carefully. He observed the customs of the people and took note of their rather peculiar system of social stratification based on hereditary caste groupings. He spoke and dressed like a Brahman, and even donned the 'sacred thread' (neck cord) symbolic of the ritual status of high-caste Hindus. In fact, he wanted to be acknowledged as some kind of Roman Brahman. He gave the Hindus a simple and straightforward but by no means insignificant message. He said to them that they would find in Christianity a nobler and more refined version of their ancestral faith and should, therefore, embrace it. He claimed the allegiance of Brahmans whose 'pure' company he sought and kept, leaving it to later Christian missionaries to appear among the lower castes, as the theatrical sannyasi, or world renouncers, who have, among other achievements, transcended the restrictions on social contact between high and low groups that the caste system enjoins upon ordinary householders. The Jesuit missionary Baltazan da Costa was such a sannyasi, and he worked among the lower castes of Madurai even while de Nobili was still there. Between them they sought to save all the Hindu souls that were there.

Given the prevailing circumstances, the success they achieved was remarkable. But the preaching of the Gospel in heathen lands has never been easy. A hundred years after Roberto de Nobili's arrival, two Lutherans arrived in the very same south-eastern part of India, in 1706, to carry on with the mission. One of them, Bartholomaeus Ziegenbalg, wrote a dozen years later, a few months before his death at the age of thirty-six: 'And since I know that my work often does not attain the looked-for goal, at times such great sorrow and sadness overtake me that I cannot comfort myself and I experience many sleepless nights. Much patience is required in order to labour tirelessly for souls and not be frightened away when the work seems useless.'[3]

Christianity was, of course, not a new religion in India. It had arrived here a millennium and a half earlier with the apostle Thomas himself, who established the Syrian Christian Church in south-western India at a time when there were no Christians in the homelands of the de Nobilis, da Costas and Zeigenbalgs. What these missionaries of the sixteenth and following centuries represented was, however, more than a religious faith: they represented a manifold expansion of Europe into Asia, Africa and Latin America, and the quest for Hinduism had many motives and many meanings depending upon who was seeking it.

By the second half of the eighteenth century the British had succeeded in driving out their European rivals from the subcontinent of India and were engaged in consolidating and expanding their trading activities. The British East India Company found it prudent to take on the responsibility of political control in the promotion of its interest in commercial enterprise. To trade profitably it had to have political control; to stabilize its political control it had to govern well. The ideas of what constituted good government in those days (of Adam Smith, Jeremy Bentham and John Stuart Mill) could be summed up as minimum interference in the life of the people. To achieve such a relationship with the governed, the governors had to systematically acquire knowledge about these ways of life. Ironically, this soon led them to negative judgements.

Inspired by Warren Hastings, the Governor-General of

[3] I am grateful to D. Dennis Hudson (Smith College, USA) for this information.

Bengal, who showed considerable interest in the revival of ancient Indian learning, Sir William Jones, the father of indology, set up the Asiatic Society at Calcutta in 1784. Under its auspices the study of ancient scriptural, legal and literary texts was inaugurated. Jones himself led with a translation of, among other texts, Kalidasa's *Shakuntala* (published in 1789) which, it has been asserted, made Indians 'hold up their heads as civilized, cultured men' (Cannon 1964: 166). Goethe's well-known paean, which he wrote on reading Jones's translation of the play, introduced German scholars to the treasure house of classical Sanskrit literature.

These scholarly activities soon came to be supplemented by the careful collection of information about the prevalent customs and practices of the peoples of India by civil servants. However, the indologists and the civil servants, it seems, did not communicate much with one another; consequently, two British images of India came to be formed. While the India of the indologists could well be proud of her ancient literary, metaphysical and religious traditions, the India of civil-servant ethnographers could only be ashamed of her lack of civilization, her superstitions and magic, her barbarian customs such as *ṭhagi* (highway robbery and murder in the name of religion), sati (immolation of the Hindu widow on her deceased husband's funeral pyre), and prostitution among the *devadāsī* (temple dancers) (see Carman 1983). One such civil servant, Charles Trevelyan, wrote in 1837:

> Almost every false religion has paid court to some of the bad passions of mankind. But neither in Greece, in Carthage, nor in Scandinavia, was superstition ever so diametrically opposed to morality as in India, at the present day. If we were to form a graduated scale of religions, that of Christ and that of Kalee (the patron goddess of the Thags) would be the opposite extremes. (Reeves 1971: 38)

Such views were readily echoed by contemporary missionaries, who, abandoning the subtle approach of the early Jesuits noted above, openly condemned Hindu customs, religious practices and beliefs as stupid, barbarian, and even inherently depraved. They discounted the suggestion that things had, in any way, been better in the past. Even such a patient and meticulous observer of Hindu customs and practices as Abbé J. A.

Dubois (he lived in south India during the closing years of the eighteenth and the first quarter of the nineteenth century), who tried to cultivate some degree of sympathy for the people he observed, could not resist announcing in the preface to his account of Hindu customs that the motive which above all others influenced his determination to publish the records of his researches was his hope 'that a faithful picture of the wickedness and incongruities of polytheism and idolatory would by its ugliness help greatly to set off the beauties and perfections of Christianity' (1906: 9).

In sharp contrast to the disgust that Hinduism generated in the hearts and minds of civil servants and missionaries was the unbounded enthusiasm of the indologists for the quality of ancient Hindu thought and literature. The most distinguished of these European indologists of the nineteenth century was Max Müller, who made the first ever translation of the Rig Veda (11th century B.C.) into a Western language, namely English. On the title-page of the translation he proclaimed his immense enthusiasm for India's ancient culture by presenting his own name, and those of his native country (Germany) and the university where he taught (Oxford), in quaint Sanskritized forms as *mokṣa mula*, *Śarmaṇa deśa* and *uksatarana* respectively. In one of his many panegyrics he wrote:

> If I were asked under what human sky the human mind has most fully developed some of its choicest gifts, has most deeply pondered on the greatest problems of life, and has found solutions of some of them which will deserve the attention even of those who have studied Plato and Kant—I should point to India. And if I were to ask myself from what literature we, here in Europe . . . may draw that corrective which is most wanted in order to make our inner life more perfect, more comprehensive, more universal, in fact more truly human, a life, not for this life only, but a transfigured and eternal life—again I should point to India (quoted in Chaudhuri 1974: 303).

But even Max Müller believed that degradation and hideousness had assailed Hinduism in his day and that Brahmanism had ceased to live more than a thousand years ago. He too, and not Charles Trevelyan alone, was horrified by Kali. He never visited India.

It should not be hard to imagine the anxieties and perplexities that the researches of indologists and ethnographers must have caused to Indians, who were being 'modernized' by English education. While they could brush aside the unqualified condemnation of civil servants and the ever-suspect Christian missionaries, they could not similarly dismiss the views and sorrows of a friend and scholar like Max Müller. The impact of Christianity on Hinduism, and more generally the encounter of European and Hindu cultures, produced acute tensions and, as often happens, out of these arose new cultural movements, predominantly reformist or revivalist, constituting the two faces of the so-called Hindu renaissance.

THE HINDU RENAISSANCE: REFORMISM, REVIVALISM

The recovery of the Hindu and Buddhist religious philosophies and literatures was perhaps the best gift which the British bestowed on the new intellectuals they brought into being in India through the medium of modern education, but this realization had to await developments in the second half of the nineteenth century. So overwhelmed were these early middle and upper class intellectuals by the superiority of Western thought and English education that one of the best-known among them, Rammohan Roy (1772–1833), protested to the Governor-General, Lord Amherst, on learning of the government's decision in 1823 to establish in Calcutta a new college for Sanskrit studies: he feared that it would 'load the minds of youth with grammatical niceties and metaphysical distinctions' of doubtful value (de Barry 1969; Vol. II, 41–3). He maintained that in opposing such education and instead advocating the promotion of 'a more liberal and enlightened system of instruction', including mathematics, natural philosophy, chemistry and 'other useful sciences', he was 'discharging a solemn duty' to his countrymen. A very learned man, well versed in his native Bengali and the Sanskrit, Persian, Arabic and English cultural and literary traditions, Rammohan had resigned from the East India Company to espouse the cause of social and moral regeneration of his people. Historians have called him 'the father of Indian recovery' and 'in fact the first modern man in India' (Panikkar 1956: 216–17; also see Joshi 1975).

He favoured Westernization, using in his writings and speeches emotive words such as 'enlightenment', amelioration', 'improvement', 'benefit', 'happiness' and so on to describe its expected results.

Rammohan operated on two fronts. Convinced of the need for the purification of the religious life of Hindus in the direction of a syncretic theism, he founded the Brahmo Sabha (association of the worshippers of God) in 1828, with a view to synthesizing what he considered to be the most valuable elements in Vedic Hinduism and Protestant Christianity. He also launched or supported campaigns for the eradication of social abuses of various kinds in Hindu society, such as child marriage, restrictions on the remarriage of widows, caste taboos and, above all, the practice of sati. He proclaimed that he found 'the doctrines of Christ more conducive to moral principles and better adapted for the use of rational beings' (de Riencourt 1961: 213) than any other he knew of. In fact, he wrote a dissertation on the moral precepts of Jesus. He became one of the prominent unitarians of his time, recognized as such in Britain and America.

Rammohan's religious philosophy was perhaps too austere and intellectual, and demanded what must have then appeared too sudden and major a break with Hinduism for it not to arouse the hostility of the orthodox Hindus or to have much widespread influence. The remarkable thing, however, is how much of Hinduism he retained alongside Christian and Islamic elements in the new unitarian Sabha, later renamed the Brahmo Samaj in 1843 by Debendranath Tagore. Quite unintended by him, perhaps, Roy's efforts to found a new religion helped to rejuvenate the flagging spirit of Hindu intellectuals, and warded off the serious threat which Christianity posed to Hinduism in his day by making a compromise with it.

The universal religion which Rammohan Roy had dreamt of really died with him. His successors were less broadminded and eclectic, leaning by turns one way or the other towards Hinduism or Christianity. However, they concerned themselves with his objectives of social reform with determination. This inevitably drew them back closer to Hindu society. Their opposition to the intrusion of Christian elements into their faith also became stronger with the passage of time. In 1865, however, the Samaj split as the younger members, led by Keshab Chandra Sen, felt disturbed by what they considered to be an excessive load of Brahmanical ritual and symbolism. Two years later, Debendranath Tagore, the principal second generation leader of the Samaj, warned his followers that they must not cut themselves off completely from 'the great Hindu community' and the 'highest truths of Hindu Shastras' (canonical texts), if they were to have any influence on other Indians. It is obvious that the battle for a new religion had been lost because it was never joined: the Brahmos never really broke away from Hinduism. It was too late in the day for Debendranath to proclaim (in the message mentioned above) 'that we are Brahmos first, and Indians or Hindus afterwards' (de Barry 1959: Vol. II, 58; also see Kopf 1979).

Rammohan Roy and his immediate followers sought a religious response to the challenge of Christianity and the West. There were other intellectuals who opted for a secular worldview, drawing inspiration from the British utilitarians and French positivists. Instead of the worship of god, they advocated the deification of man in the name of secular humanism, and cultivated rationalism and scientism. In this struggle between theism and humanism, between faith and reason, it was religion which always retained the upper hand (see Kopf 1979).

While the Brahmos split, with some of them led by Keshab Chandra Sen drawing closer to the teachings of Jesus and even striving for an Indian version of Christianity, and the positivists held their debates and the annual festival in honour of Auguste Comte, Hindu Bengal turned its gaze in admiration and reverence on Sri Ramakrishna (1836–86), a unique religious mystic who wanted to 'find out everything himself, empirically'. Even Keshab Sen paid obeisance to him. A simple rustic priest at the temple of Kali at Dakshineshvar on the banks of the Ganga near Calcutta, he was not an intellectual but possessed of the intensest love and longing for the goddess whose worship was his appointed duty and natural inclination. In course of time, he flowered into a saint and mystic of incomparable quality. Ramakrishna was little concerned with society at large. Like Rammohan Roy, he too was interested in the synthesis of religions, not on the intellectual but the emotional plane. He lived during different phases of his spiritual quest as a Christian and Muslim but always returned to Hinduism, emphasizing the unity of all religious experience. By all accounts he achieved his personal goal of 'god-realization' (see Isherwood 1965). The issue, from the point of view of Hindu society, was how to make people in the far-flung corners of the country share in this miracle.

After the death of Keshab Sen in 1884 the Brahmo Samaj lay split and shattered. Ramakrishna's message of love of God and man was yet confined to his immediate circle of disciples and admirers. One of these, Swami Vivekananda (1863–1902), was a very unusual man. He came under the master's spell when he was eighteen years old and died at the age of thirty-nine. However, by then he had not only succeeded in spreading a new awareness of the need for purifying their religious and social life among Hindus all over India; he had also carried the message of Hinduism abroad, to the United States and to Great Britain. Vivekananda was a man with a mission and in a frantic hurry. He was always on the offensive, both at home and abroad. Contemporary accounts of the World Parliament of Religions, held in Chicago in 1893, reveal that he was its most impressive and eloquent participant.

Vivekananda found much to criticize in Hindu society. He condemned the Hindus' excessive ritualism, their indifference to human misery and poverty, and the constrictive and divisive influence of the caste system. To set things right, he advocated the cultivation of self-confidence and self-criticism: 'No religion on earth preaches the dignity of humanity in such lofty strains as Hinduism, and no religion on earth treads upon the necks of the poor and the low in such a fashion as Hinduism' (de Riencourt 1961: 245).

Vivekananda was distressed by the uncritical admiration of everything of Western origin among the Indian educated classes. He reviled it as 'base imitation', 'slavish weakness', 'disgraceful cowardice', and disdainfully asked if it was 'with these provisions only' that Indians hoped to 'scale the highest pinnacle of civilization and greatness'. He exhorted his countrymen to seek, above all, '*manliness*' (de Barry 1959: Vol. II, 103–7), thus playing the role of the counter-player which colonialism generated wherever it creeped (see Nandy 1983). He advocated the supremacy of Upanishadic philosophy and dismissed the rest as dross, but gave an interesting twist to the argument:

All our present-day religions, however crude some of them may appear to be, however inexplicable some of their purposes may seem, one who understands them and studies them can trace them back to the ideas of Upanishads. . . . Great spiritual and philosophical ideas in the Upanishads are today with us, converted into household worship in the form of symbols. (Panikkar 1963: 31)

As a religious teacher Vivekananda was a puritanical reformer and a revivalist; he was an apologist, though an aggressive one, and inevitably a propagandist. He repeatedly emphasized that the West was the victim of its materialist outlook and India's spiritual ideas alone could save it. Therefore, the great ideal to which he asked Indians to dedicate themselves was 'the conquest of the whole world by India—nothing less than that'. In India, he advocated the service and the uplift of the exploited and the poor in the spirit of sacrifice and love of mankind: 'they alone live who live for others' (de Barry 1959: Vol. II, 100, 103). This was practical Vedanta. Watching from distant Oxford, Max Müller, for whom Vivekananda had high admiration (he realized that the revival he was endeavouring to bring about had been greatly helped by the work of indologists), felt disturbed by the mixing up of Vedanta (the way of knowledge) and the devotional mysticism of Ramakrishna (the way of love). He wished the efforts of the Hindu reformer and his collaborators well so long as they kept true to Vedanta (Chaudhuri 1974: 329). Events took a different course, however.

It is not Vivekananda's fiery rhetoric so much that survives today as his world-wide Ramakrishna Mission centres for devoted public service in the fields of education, medical relief and religious instruction (see Nikhilananda 1953). In India there are over a hundred such centres, symbolizing the reformulation of abstract Vedantic ideas into concrete moral practice. The transformation of an autological religion of personal salvation through world renunciation into a vehicle of altruistic service was Vivekananda's principal contribution to the social-cultural history of the India of his times. This transformation is not to be understood in terms of the Weberian concept of an expanding rationality, or merely as a response to the challenge of the West: it has deeper indigenous roots (Gupta 1974: 25–50).

From Rammohan Roy to Vivekananda, it was Bengal which was in the forefront of the so-called Hindu renaissance. The rest of India was not, however, quiescent. In fact, Maharashtra contributed in a major way to Hindu social and religious reform. Mahadev Govind Ranade (1841–1901) was one more of those titans which nineteenth-century India produced. Assuming leadership of the Prarthana Samaj ('Prayer Society'), which was established in 1867 at Poona, and echoing the aspirations of the Brahmo Samaj (Keshab Chander Sen visited the city in 1864), he tried to give its programme a broad scope. Firmly rooted in Hinduism, the Prarthana Samaj looked forward to reforming Hindu society (widow remarriage, intercaste marriage, abolition of infant marriage and of the practice of dowry-giving were notable activities in their programme) and giving a forward-looking orientation to Hinduism. Influenced by Herbert Spencer's theory of social evolution, Ranade wrote in 1872 of his conviction that 'a universal kingdom of God on earth below' would replace 'sectional churches' (see Kellock 1926: 166), for all religions were evolving towards 'pure theism'. In consonance with his ideas on religious evolution, his proposals for social reform were explicitly a repudiation of the notion that old was gold and that India needed to revive ancient traditions to move forward. He wrote: 'It seems to be forgotten that in a living organism, as society is, no revival is possible. The dead and the buried or burnt are dead, buried and burnt once for all, and the dead past cannot, therefore, be revived except by a reformation of the old materials into new organized beings' (de Barry 1958: Vol. II, 132). Though Ranade himself moved from success to success in his own wide-ranging, glittering career, the Prarthana Samaj failed to achieve any comparable successes. It was a yet another frankly revivalist Hindu movement, which Ranade did not approve of, that was to have a marked impact upon Hindus.

Hindu revivalism found its most uncompromising exponent in the Gujarati scholar and sannyasi, Dayananda Sarasvati (1824–83). His call was for a return to the Vedas and a total rejection of all other religions. He published a vitriolic attack on Christianity, Islam and post-Buddhist Hinduism in a crudely fanciful but forceful book *Satyartha Prakash* (The light of truth). He attacked idol worship, excessive ritualism, untouchability, child marriage, the subjection of women and other evils that, in his view, had corrupted Hindu religion and society. He founded the Arya Samaj (the society of 'noble men') in 1875. He also made the cow a central unifying symbol of Hindu society, deriving its holiness from Hindu mythology. Dayananda stressed the importance of education and social service, and blessed the idea of conversion of non-Hindus to Hinduism. This and his other ideas gave him an immense following in western and northern India, particularly in Panjab (see Jordens 1978).

These revivalist movements and the work of indologists found a distorted echo in the so-called Theosophical Movement of the Polish countess, Madame Blavatsky. Though obviously quite ignorant of Hindu and Buddhist religious literature, she became a self-appointed cultural ambassador, proclaiming the superiority of Indian thought over European philosophies. She had some temporary connection with Dayananda but he broke off with her. Her followers, notably Annie Besant, were perhaps better acquainted with Indian religions: at any rate, they were able to win a following among credulous educated Indians, mixing metaphysical ideas with occultism, much to the dismay of a true savant like Max Müller. The sociological significance of the movement, however, was that it helped restore among those Hindus who were influenced by it a respect for their own religious tradition.

The militancy of Dayananda and the self-confidence of Vivekananda were soon to have implications outside the domain of social and cultural reformism and revivalism—in the arena of politics. Though the Arya Samaj and the Ramakrishna Mission disclaimed political interests, their impact on Hindu political leaders and the masses had been so widespread that a linkage between religious revivalism and nationalism was inevitable; and that is what actually happened, despite Vivekananda's warning that if India gave up the religious quest in favour of politics she would die (de Riencourt 1961: 250).

HINDUISM, NATIONALISM AND COMMUNALISM

Rammohan Roy had great faith in the advantages of British rule and hoped for a socio-cultural and religious renaissance under its auspices, for he saw in it a civilizing force. 'India needs many more years of British domination', he wrote (de Riencourt 1961: 230). Little did he realize that, within a few decades of his death, a resurgent Hindusim would begin to sprout political ambitions and strive to oust the British from India.

An important element in the political awakening of India was a growing liberalism in Europe itself. Education through the medium of English, modelled after British schools and colleges, became the principal vehicle of this influence. Understandably, it was in Indian literatures that the nationalist urges of the English-educated classes found their first utterance. In this connection, the name that comes to mind above all others is that of the Bengali littérateur, Bankimchandra Chatterji (1838–94). His famous novel *Ananda Matha*, published in 1876, gave pointed expression to the Hindu aversion to aliens (*mleccha*), whether Muslim or British, and the opposition to their cultural and political domination of India. It contained the famous Sanskrit poem *Vande mātaram* (I bow to thee, Mother!) (see Das 1984: 228–9 for the full text and English translation), which identified India with the supreme mother goddess—a hymn which not only became the national song during the freedom movement under the leadership of the Indian National Congress, but also initiated the use of Hindu religious symbolism in modern Indian politics. India became *Bhārat Mātā*, Mother India.

The Indian National Congress was, as is well known, founded by, among others, a retired British civil servant, Allan Hume (in 1885), with moderate political goals; its membership had nothing to do with religion. Its president in 1887 was a Mussim, Badruddin Tyabji. The organization was, nevertheless, dominated by Hindus, and the number of Muslim delegates attending its annual sessions, which never exceeded 25 per cent of all delegates, fell from year to year. The attitude of Muslim Congressmen as well as that of their co-religionists who remained outside it was influenced by a factional power struggle within the Congress. The 'moderates', who, though not devoid of religious faith in their personal lives, maintained a secular stance in politics, finally lost to the 'extremists' led by the Bengali Aurobindo Ghose and the Maharashtrian Bal Gangadhar Tilak. Tilak combined the Western ideas of nationalism and patriotism with an activist interpretation of the religious philosphy of Hinduism. Ghose proclaimed: 'Nationalism is not a mere political programme; nationalism is a religion that has come from God' (de Barry 1959: Vol. II, 727).

Bal Gangadhar Tilak (1856–1920) played a particularly notable part in weaving together Hindu nationalist and religious sentiments. He recruited the Hindu god Ganapati to the national movement by skilfully converting a popular ten-day annual religious festival in his honour into the occasion for intensified anti-British propaganda in an atmosphere of fervid religious enthusiasm (see Cashman 1975). The 'holy' cow was even more deeply involved in politics than before by combining an anti-cow-killing agitation with the larger political goals. The seventeenth-century Maratha hero Shivaji, who had challenged the Mughal empire, was also honoured with a festival. Appeal to Hindu religious sentiment undoubtedly helped to draw Hindus together on an all-India level, but it also alienated the Muslims (Smith 1963: 87–94; Dumont 1970: 89–110). Originating in a complex historical situation, Muslim separatism was strengthened by the manner in which the Congress developed its campaign against British rule by emphasizing Hindu solidarity. Ultimately, coinciding with the growing assertiveness of the 'extremist' elements, a group of Muslim leaders founded the Muslim League in 1906 with the blessings of the British Government of India. The seal was placed on this act of separation by the British Parliament's India Councils Act of 1909, which provided for separate electorates (Smith 1963: 84–7).

The leadership of the Congress passed into the hands of M. K. Gandhi (1869–1948) on the death of Tilak in 1920. In 1915, while the militant Tilak was still the dominant personality on the Indian scene, Gandhi said he wanted to spiritualize politics, which meant for him the re-establishment of an imperative link between moral values and secular interests. When Tilak wrote to him that politics was a game of worldly people, and not of sadhus, Gandhi replied: 'For me there is no conflict. . . . I venture to say that it betrays mental laziness to think that the world is not for *sadhus*' (Iyer 1973: 50). He explained further in his autobiography: 'To see the universal and all-pervading spirit of Truth face to face . . . a man who aspires after that cannot afford to keep out of any field of life. That is why my devotion to Truth has drawn me into the field of politics; . . . *those who say that religion has nothing to do with politics do not know what religion means*' (Gandhi 1927: 615, emphasis added).

Again, late in his life when beginning to get into the thick of his last great compaign against British imperialism in India in 1940, he reaffirmed: 'I still hold the view that I cannot conceive of politics as divorced from religion. Indeed religion should pervade every one of our actions. Here religion does not mean sectarianism. . . . This religion transcends Hinduism, Islam, Christianity, etc. It does not supersede them. It harmonizes them and gives them reality' (Gandhi 1984: 54).

Mahatma Gandhi genuinely respected all religions and his outlook on life was influenced by Jainism and Christianity and Islam. Though he considered all religions to be equally true, and equally imperfect, the 'centre of his being', in the words of his admiring Christian friend Charles Andrews, ever remained firmly 'fixed in Hinduism' (Bondurant 1959: 121). Being so convinced, he considered religious conversion as an expression of lack of genuine religious faith, and was horrified by religious conflict. He said: 'Religion is outraged when an outrage is perpetrated in its name' (Gandhi 1961: 47). He set out not only to cleanse Hinduism of its ugly aspects (most strikingly the practice of untouchability) but also to build mutual goodwill and respect among the adherents of the many religions of India. To take the national movement out of the 'drawing-rooms' of the educated middle classes and make it a mass movement inevitably meant Hinduizing it too, given the predominance of Hindus in the country's population. He used such expressions as *daridra-nārāyaṇa* (God is the poor, or the poor are God),[4] *harijan* (the people of God) to refer to Hindu untouchables, and *rāma-*

[4] Compare this with Gandhi's famous statement: 'To a people famishing and idle, the only acceptable form in which god can dare appear is work and promise of food as wages' (de Barry 1959: Vol. II, 268).

rājya (God's kingdom) to visualize the independent India of his dreams. On their part, the masses responded to Gandhi as a *māhātmā*, a man of religion, a holy person with spiritual attainments and even magical powers (see Amin 1984).

Gandhi's effort to unite Hindus and Muslims in the pursuit of the national goal of independence failed in the end. Extremist elements among Hindus and Muslims alike repudiated his leadership: to the former he was a foe of Hinduism, to the latter, of their political aspiration for separation. The Congress continued to count Muslims among its followers, but the Muslim League demanded in 1940 a separate homeland for Indian Muslims to be carved out of the subcontinent. Hindu opposition to this demand was voiced under the leadership of the exclusive political party, the Hindu Mahasabha, and the militant socio-religious organization called the Rashtriya Swayamsevak Sangh (Smith 1963). Nationalism in India became polarized, with Hindus and Muslims generally pitted against each other, and, though most Hindus stayed with the Congress, the two turbulent streams of communalism flowed along their separate courses, as the subcontinent lurched forward towards independence. Communalism in the sense of the conduct of struggle for independence and power on the basis of religious identity rather than the principle of territory—the usual basis of nationalism—thus came to dominate the internal politics of India.

Gandhi and the Congress could not stem the tide of communalism. India was partitioned in the middle of 1947 and the Islamic state of Pakistan was born in the midst of communal riots on an unprecedented scale, resulting in the killing of thousands of Hindus, Muslims and Sikhs in many parts of the subcontinent, but most of all in Bengal and Panjab. Millions became refugees and crossed the newly created international frontiers. Gandhi was in deep anguish; his life's work lay in a shambles. He did not have to suffer long as he was assassinated early in 1948 by a group of Hindu conspirators owing allegiance to the Hindu militant parties (see Nandy 1980).

Instead of cleansing politics of its unsavoury aspects, as men of faith such as Mahatma Gandhi and his great contemporary, the littérateur, philosopher and Nobel Laureate Rabindranath Tagore (1861–1941), had believed it would, religion, reduced in the political arena to a mere 'sign' of distinction between human groups, a 'shadow' of itself (Dumont 1970: 90–1), in the end fouled politics.

INDEPENDENCE, SECULARISM AND MODERNIZATION

Jawaharlal Nehru (1889–1964) committed independent India to the custody of a modern secular state with the principal task of modernizing the country through the application of science and technology for the removal of ignorance, ill health and poverty. Or so he hoped he could do. Nehru was a modernizer, but he was by no means against religion as such: he was, however, deeply conscious of the harm which religiosity had done in India. Confined to prison, he had written just three years before he became the Prime Minister of free India in 1947 that it was 'with the temper and approach of science, allied to philosophy, and with reverence for all that lies beyond' that Indians 'must face life'. He had further stressed:

> India must therefore lessen her religiosity and turn to science. She must get rid of the exclusiveness in thought and social habit which has become like a prison to her, stunting her spirit and preventing her growth. . . . The day-to-day religion of the orthodox Hindu is more concerned with what to eat, who to eat with and from whom to keep away, than with spiritual values. . . . The Moslem . . . has his own narrow codes and ceremonials, a routine which he vigorously follows, forgetting the lesson of brotherhood which his religion taught him. (1961: 547)

Nehru lost no time in having a very detailed constitution framed for free India and it was inaugurated in 1950. The ideal of secularism was clearly embodied in the document; the main relevant clause guaranteed 'freedom of conscience and free profession, practice and propagation of religion' (Article 28). Religion was not debarred from public life but dissociated from the state, which was required to treat followers of all religions equally, favouring or disfavouring no citizen on the ground of his faith. Secularization in India does not mean privatization of religion; nor does it mean that the state will have nothing to do with the religious life of the people. To take but one example, when upwards of ten million people converge at a place of pilgrimage, as they do at Prayag on the occasion of the *kumbha* (an astrological event of periodic occurrence), the government may not disown responsibility for running special trains, making appropriate arrangements for the protection of public health and the maintenance of law and order.

Political scientists seem to be generally agreed that, unfavourable circumstances notwithstanding, the governance of free India has been largely free of religious intolerance. They even venture the opinion that Hinduism is 'on the whole favourable to the development of a secular state' and draw attention to 'its strong tradition of freedom of conscience and tolerance of religious diversity' (Smith 1963: 493). It is also pointed out by some scholars, who believe that the dissociation of the secular from the spiritual components of Indian civilization took place a long time ago, that the temporal-eccelesiastical feuds characteristic of the history of the West did not occur here. On the contrary, there has been 'a constant interplay and cross-cutting between these two polarities' (Kothari 1970: 251).

Other students of Indian history arrive at a similar conclusion about the contemporary situation but along different lines of argument. Thus, A. K. Saran, a contemporary Hindu social philosopher, writes:

> The step from religious fanaticism, corruption and persecution to science and technology which the West took, and which was unique and significant in being a solution not so much *against* as *outside* religion and faith, was a step not taken in India independently of the Western encounter and conquest. While in this sense it is external, it is internal in the sense that it is part of India's history, as also of the history of Hindu tradition. (1972: 32)

Most analysts seem to concur, however, that the secular state in India cannot be taken for granted, and that the major threat it has faced since independence is from Hindu communalism. The situation has become complicated in recent years through the renewed salience of Muslim and Sikh communalism in national and regional politics. It is obvious that India's religious traditions do not provide the same congenial setting for a separation of the state and the church—Hinduism and Islam have no Church and Sikhism alone may be said to have in the

Gurudwara an institution comparable to the Church—which prevailed in the setting of the Christian tradition in Europe. In fact—and as already stated—the situation in India is so critically different that secularism here entails positive responsibilities for the state, to be discharged without discrimination in respect of the different religious communities.

The 'secular' and 'socialist' state that has been established in India has, as its major goal, the removal of the poverty of the masses. The principal means to this end has been planning for economic and social development. Nehru, with his Fabian socialist ideas and admiration for the positive achievements of the Soviet Union, had prepared the Congress party and the country's elites for such a course of action years before he came to power. A debate that almost inevitably came to be raised in this connection was with regard to the role of Hinduism: would it impede economic and social development?

Apologists of British rule as well as its critics had long argued that India had remained a backward country because of its religious values and constrictive social structure. The argument had been initiated by Western scholars of the nineteenth century including, notably, Karl Marx, who saw in Hinduism a religion of extremes, 'of the Lingam, and of the Juggernaut; the religion of the Monk, and of the Bayadere' (Marx 1853). His lament about the degradation of the Hindu who, forgetful of man's position at the apex of creation, worships the cow and the monkey, is too well known to be quoted here at length. In any case, religion, in his view, could not be the root cause of India's socio-economic backwardness: this had to be traced to a particular mode of production.

It was Max Weber who presented the most detailed thesis on the subject in the early years of the twentieth century (see Weber 1958). Weber argued that the Hindu metaphysical notions of *saṁsāra* (transmigration of the soul) and *karma* (retribution in one's present incarnation for the good and bad deeds of the previous life) produced an other-worldly ethic of conduct which had not been conducive to the acquisitive drive essential for the accumulation and investment of capital. The non-innovative character of hereditary caste occupations combined with the religious doctrines to produce a traditionalistic and anti-rational culture and a social order in which there was no room for radical change. In fact, the highest merit came to be attached to a strict adherence to tradition, including caste-based duties, and any deviation from this was regarded as ritually degrading. The ' "spirit" of the whole system was incapable of giving birth to economic and technical revolutions from within itself or even of facilitating the first germination of capitalism in its midst' (Weber 1958: 112). But he thought it necessary to qualify this judgement by saying that such effects must be 'inferred' rather than 'inductively assessed'. Also, unlike Marx, he did not ask India to see its future in the image of the West (about the future of which he had grave misgivings).

Weber's thesis has been restated in one form or another by many scholars, a recent example being Myrdal's critique of traditional Hindu social structure (Myrdal 1968). He does not, however, pay much attention to religious values, asserting that, though religion has nowhere in southern Asia induced social change, the basic doctrines of Hinduism (and other religions of the region) are not necessarily inimical to modernization. Several other social scientists, most notably Milton Singer, have examined Weber's thesis in the light of empirical evidence regarding social change and found little support for it. Indeed, Singer (1972: 272–373) points out that Weber himself wrote about the adaptive nature of the caste system in the context of the industrialization of the country. His mistake obviously was that he confused ideal-types with empirical realities and took a thoroughly ethnocentric, and therefore misleading view of Hindu religion and society. He overemphasized the conservative effects of the religious ideology on Hindu society, and did not pay enough heed to the influence which a changing socio-economic order could have, and in fact has had, on Hindu religious belief.

Singer proceeds to develop his notion of 'compartmentalization' of Hindu society, describing the empirical process of the separation of 'spheres of conduct and belief that would otherwise collide' (1972: 321), and the consequent 'ritual neutralization of the work sphere' (p. 325), and 'vicarious ritualization' (p. 331). The latter process involves the abridgement of rituals, or their performance by proxy, but not their total abandonment, on the part of the industrial entrepreneurs in Madras whose life-style Singer studied.

These conclusions find support from researches carried out in other parts of the country. The obstructive role of Hinduism in the 'modernization' of India is not a live sociological issue any more. As Morris David Morris put it twenty-five years ago, 'there is no precise definition of a "Hindu value system" that can be identified as a significant obstacle to economic growth or change' (1960: 607). It may be argued, however, that contemporary Hinduism is but the ruins of a once-living religious faith, which was fundamentally averse to the kind of values subsumed under modernity (Saran 1963: 87–94).

CONCLUDING REMARKS: THE QUEST FOR HINDUISM

Since its encounter with Christianity early in the seventeenth century, Hinduism has never been disengaged from the West in the consciousness of 'modern' Hindus, and it is their predicament that I have tried to describe here. Today the challenge that Hinduism faces does not come from an alien religion but from the Western ideals of secularism and modernization. It is not suggested that prior to this encounter Hinduism had experienced no internal schisms and change or no external threat. Buddhism and Islam are writ too large on the pages of South and South-east Asian history for such a view to be entertained. This epilogue itself has been partly concerned with the political consequences in the twentieth century of the ideological cleavage which the coming of Islam produced among the the peoples of the subcontinent. The cultural synthesis between Hinduism and Islam, which the pre-Partition opponents eloquently wrote and spoke about, remained confined to frills—undoubtedly important as such but still frills—such as art and architecture (Mukerji 1947: 31–60). Muslim sufism (mysticism) and Sikhism did represent creative developments arising out of the prolonged coexistence of Hindus and Muslims in India. The sufi remained passive, however, dwelling on the outskirts of society, as it were; and the Sikhs, first persecuted by Muslim kings, later developed political ambitions, which made them the foes of Muslims. In short, implicit in the approach adopted here is the conviction that, at the macro-level, the history of Hinduism constitutes also its sociology.

The historical approach has been advocated also by the propagandists of Hinduism, but more as an expression of hope than in an effort to understand what they themselves observed.

> If Hinduism lives today, it is due to [the central principles of the faith], but it lives so little. . . . Hinduism is a movement, not a position; a process, not a result; a growing tradition, not a fixed revelation. Its past history encourages us to believe that it will be found equal to any emergency that the future may throw up, whether on the field of thought or of history. (Radhakrishnan 1927: 128, 129–30)

One would have thought that events since the above was written, more than half a century ago, had decisively disproved the everlasting viability of traditional Hinduism; but the apologists survive and are confident that Western science and technology do not pose any threat to their faith (see, for example, Devaraja 1975). This confidence is, in fact, only naivety, when it is not a posture, for modern science, as philosophy and as technology, is fundamentally opposed to all religions.

It is not at all surprising, therefore, that 'modern' Hindus today live more on strategies than by faith—that Hinduism in the lives of its adherents increasingly incorporates compromises. This is understandably more true of urban-educated Hindus than of illiterate villagers. Leading Hindu scientists, who have become well known to newspaper readers thanks to their achievements in the fields of nuclear fission and space exploration, call for salvage operations, to rediscover what is precious in Hindu and Buddhist thought.[5] There are others who would like to vindicate Hinduism by bringing out the compatibility of Hindu mythology with scientific knowledge.[6] Such 'ideological

[5] Dr Raja Ramanna, Director of the Bhabha Atomic Research Centre, Bombay, has said in public that he believes that much 'scientific knowledge' is to be found in Sanskrit works if only modern scientists correctly interpret them. 'He suggested that higher mathematics and quantum mechnanics raised the same questions which the Buddhist and Hindu mystical sciences tried to answer.' *The Times of India* (New Delhi), 25 April 1976.

[6] I heard a leading exponent of Indian classical dance explain the dance item *daśa-avatāra* (ten incarnations of god) to a mixed audience of Indians and foreigners at Delhi University in 1975. She maintained that the notion of *avatāra* was in harmony with the theory of evolution. Some years earlier, I had heard a famous Indo-Anglian poet make the same point before an audience at an American University; in fact, he went further and said that the notion was in harmony with both the theory of evolution and the Marxist view of historical development.

rigour' is, however, invariably accompanied by 'ritualistic tolerance' among modern Hindus everywhere, in India and abroad (see Bharati 1976, and Pocock 1973 and 1976).

The concern of the 'modern' Hindu with instant religious experience in the midst of his other activities makes him shy away from a slow-moving ritual-ridden life and its guardians, the priests, in the direction of the sadhu (saintly person) and the guru (religious preceptor), who may even perform miracles. It is thus that he reassures himself of his identity as a Hindu. It is important to note that his need for such reassurance is not to be confused with the guru-hunting of Western, particularly American, youth. Whereas the Hindu wants to cling to his past, to his tradition from which he is becoming alienated, American youth seek an alternative to its secular culture as well as to the established religions and anti-religious philosophies associated with that culture. The Hare Krishna devotees, for example, are protesting as much against American culture as against such counter-culture movements as derive their inspiration from within Western culture itself (Judah 1974; Brent 1973).

'Modern' Hindus, though only a small fraction of the total Hindu population, provide leadership not only to their community in social and religious matters, but also in diverse fields of national concern. It is unlikely that they will do now what Mahatma Gandhi failed to persuade them do in his lifetime—turn away from the unthinking rush to modernization. They also hope somehow to retain their Hindu identity, appealing to a vaunted tradition of eclecticism, unmindful of the fact that it has been essentially sterile, a sign of doubt more than of anything else. In the circumstances they lead fragmented lives—the very denial of a mode of living having its roots in religion. The caste system, Hinduism's steel frame, is badly fractured, and not in urban areas only. The spheres in which the fundamental notions of ritual purity and impurity still apply are shrinking fast. Caste loyalties are put to new uses, such as winning elections. The Hindu conception of cyclical time has been overwhelmed by Western linear time, and the new watchword

---

Bharati (1970) calls this the modern apologetic of the Hindu renaissance: the harnessing of 'technological simile and parable to vindicate or exemplify ancient truths' (p. 268).

is, of course, progress. Hinduism seemingly survives, but not undisturbed, in the daily lives of millions of ordinary Indians (see, for example, Pocock 1973; Babb 1975; Wadley 1975). There is, however, something oppressively mechanical about it which colourful fairs and festivals, domestic rituals and distant pilgrimages, even the sadhu and the guru do not quite help to relieve except momentarily. The vital sources of thought and emotional experience seem to have presently dried up, and what survives is, perhaps, ruins, though this may not be the view offered to those who live in them.

Mahatma Gandhi saw very clearly the conflict between Hindu tradition and Western civilization, and so did Jawaharlal Nehru, but from the opposite end. And Nehru was the typical 'modern' Indian. The wistfulness of his response to André Malraux's observation, quoted at the beginning of this epilogue, was an expression of the modern Hindu's anxiety and hope. India without Hinduism is inconceivable, but, given the present national commitment to secularism, science and technology, an infinite pause seems to have settled on Hinduism: but it is not dead. It seems to be like those rivers of Hindu mythology that flow underground but may yet rise again in full tide. Or, to borrow Mahatma Gandhi's metaphor, the Ganga may flow pure and clean again. Many Hindus, in fact, wait for such a happening. Like the Brahman anti-hero of the widely acclaimed Kannada novel *Samskara* (Anantha Murthy 1976), they wait—anxious and expectant. Others are less hopeful, for they fear that we live in a runaway world in which man has installed himself as his own god. Not that gods are all that essential in one's quest for Hinduism, but faith and understanding always were and are—even for our brave, new, modern world.

APPENDIX

A NOTE ON THE EPIGRAPHS

Throughout the book certain quotations have been used as epigraphs at the beginning of each chapter, and of the Introduction and the Epilogue. The sources of the quotations are given below.

INTRODUCTION. The quotation from Kalidasa (fifth century A.D.) is from the prologue to Act I of *Abhijnanshakuntala*. The translation is by Barbara Stoler Miller (1984: 89). The context is, of course, the staging of a play, but should also apply to the interpretation of cultures.

The admonition by Horace (65–8 B.C.) on the limitations of human knowledge is the well-known *nec scire fas est omnia* (*Odes IV*, iv. 22).

The line from T. S. Eliot (1888–1965) occurs in *East Coker*.

CHAPTER 1. Krishna Razdan (1850–1925), a Kashmiri Brahman, is remembered for his devotional poems which are sung to this day. The translation is by Nilla Cram Cook (1958: 137).

The celebration of the 'bonds of delight' is by Rabindranath Tagore (1861–1941) from song 73 of *Gitanjali* (see Tagore 1955: 34).

CHAPTER 2. This statement by a learned Kashmiri Pandit was made in answer to a question of mine regarding the significance of auspiciousness. It is worth pointing out that he managed to weave ingeniously into his statement the meaning of the *Gāyatrī mantra*, one of the holiest incantations of the Hindus, found in the Rig, Sama and Yajur Vedas, hearing which is considered both auspicious and purifying. Every Hindu who goes through the rites of ritual initiation into the status of a 'twice-born' *dvija* hears this mantra for the first time on that occasion and is expected to recite it every morning, preferably facing the sun, thereafter.

CHAPTER 3. The translation from a poem by Bhartrihari (fifth century A.D.) is by Barbara Stoler Miller (1978: 91).

The quotation from the Bhagavad Gita is from verse 45 of Chapter II.

CHAPTER 4. The quotation from the Katha Upanishad is from verse 1, section 2, of Chapter 1 in Radhakrishnan's translation (see Radhakrishnan 1953: 607).

The extract from J. Krishnamurti (1895–1986) has been taken from Vas (1973: 208).

CHAPTER 5. The quotation from the Katha Upanishad is from verse 29, section 2, of Chapter 1 in Radhakrishnan's translation (1953: 607).

The second quotation is from the 'sayings' (*vākya*) of Lal Ded, a fourteenth-century Shaivite mystic poetess of Kashmir. The translation is by Kaul (1973: 123).

EPILOGUE. Bankimchandra Chatterji (1838–94) is quoted from Bagal (1969: 231); Mahatma Gandhi (1869–1948) from Bose (1948: 261); and Jawaharlal Nehru (1889–1964) from Malraux (1968: 245–6).

REFERENCES

Amin, Shahid. 1984. 'Gandhi as Mahatma'. In Ranajit Guha, ed., *Subaltern studies III: Writings on south Asian history and society*. Delhi: Oxford University Press.

Anantha Murthy, U. R. 1976. *Samskara: A rite for a dead man*. Tr. into English from Kannada by A. K. Ramanujan. Delhi: Oxford University Press.

Ardener, Shirley. 1977. Introduction. In Shirley Ardener, ed., *Perceiving women*, pp. vii–xxiii. London: Dent & Sons Ltd.

Arieti, Silvano. 1972. *The will to be human*. New York: Quadrangle Books.

Aurobindo, Śri. 1950. *Essays on the Gita*. New York: Sri Aurobindo Library.

Austin, J. L. 1962. *Sense and sensibilia*. London: Oxford University Press.

Babb, L. A. 1975. *The divine hierarchy: Popular Hinduism in central India*. New York: Columbia University Press.

Bagal, J. C., ed. 1969. *Bankim-rachanavali*. Calcutta: Sahitya Samsad.

Bamzai, P. N. K. 1962. *A history of Kashmir*. Delhi: Metropolitan Books.

Bateson, Mary Catherine. 1984. *With a daughter's eye: A memoir of Margaret Mead and Gregory Bateson*. New York: Wm Morrow and Co.

Berger, Morroe. 1977. *Real and imagined worlds*. Cambridge, Mass.: Harvard University Press.

———. 1978. *Real and imagined worlds: The novel and social science*. Cambridge, Mass.: Harvard University Press.

Berger, Peter L. and Thomas Luckman. 1967. *The social construction of reality*. London: Allen Lane.

Berreman, G. D. 1963. *Hindus of the Himalayas*. Berkeley: University of California Press.

Bettelheim, Bruno. 1961. *The informed heart: The human condition in modern society*. London: Thames and Hudson.

Bhaduri, Sadananda. 1947. *Studies in nyāya-vaisheshika metaphysics*. Poona: Bhandarkar Oriental Research Institute.

Bharati, Agehananda. 1970. 'The Hindu renaissance and its apologetic patterns'. *The Journal of Asian Studies*, 29: 267–87.

——— 1976. 'Ritualistic tolerance and ideological rigour: Paradigm of expatriate Hindus in East Africa'. *Contributions to Indian Sociology* (n.s.), 10: 293–316.

Bondurant, J. A. 1959. *Conquest of violence: The Gandhian philosophy of conflict*. Bombay: Oxford University Press.

Bose, N. K., ed. 1984. *Selections from Gandhi*. Ahmedabad: Navjivan.

Brent, P. 1973. *Godmen of India*. Harmondsworth: Penguin Books.

Brown, Norman O. 1959. *Life against death: The psychoanalytical meaning of history*. London: Routledge and Kegan Paul.

Bühler, G. 1964. *The laws of Manu*. Delhi: Motilal Banarsidass.

Cannon, G. 1964. *Oriental Jones*. Bombay: Asia Publishing House.

Carman, John Braisted. 1974. *The theology of Ramanuja: An essay in interreligious understanding*. New Haven: Yale University Press.

———. 1983. 'The ethics of auspiciousness: Western encounter with Hindu values'. In Leroy S. Rouner, ed., *Foundations of ethics*, pp. 167–83. Notre Dame: University of Notre Dame Press.

Carman, John B. and Frédérique A. Marglin, eds. 1985. *Auspiciousness and purity*. Leiden: E. J. Brill.

Cashman, Richerd I. 1975. *The myth of the Lokamanya: Tilak and mass politics in Maharashtra*. Berkeley: University of California Press.

Chatterji, J. C. 1914. *Kashmir Shaivaism*. Srinagar: Research Department, Kashmir State.

Chaudhuri, N. C. 1974. *Scholar extraordinary: The life of Professor the Rt. Hon. Friedrich Max Müller*. Delhi: Oxford University Press.

———. 1979. *Hinduism: A religion to live by*. London: Chatto and Windus.

Cook, Nilla Cram. 1958. *The way of the swan: Poems of Kashmir*. Bombay: Asia Publishing House.

Das, Sisir Kumar. 1984. *The artist in chains: The life of Bankimchandra Chatterji*. New Delhi: New Statesman Publishing Co.

Das, Veena. 1982. *Structure and cognition: Aspects of Hindu caste and ritual*. Delhi: Oxford University Press.

de Barry, W. T., ed. 1958. *Sources of Indian tradition*. Vol. II. (Compiled by Stephen N. Hay and I. H. Qureshi.) New York: Columbia University Press.

de Riencourt, A. 1961. *The soul of India*. London: Jonathan Cape.

Devaraja, N. K. 1975. *Hinduism and the modern age*. New Delhi: Islam and Modern Age Society.

Dubois, J. A. 1906. *Hindu manners, customs and ceremonies*. (English translation by H. K. Beauchamp). Oxford: Clarendon Press.

Dumont, Louis. 1957. 'For a sociology of India'. *Contributions to India Sociology*, 1: 7–22. (Reprinted in Dumont 1970 and 1980.)

———. 1960. 'World renunciation in Indian religions'. *Contributions to Indian Sociology*, 9: 67–89.

———. 1970. *Religion, politics and history in India*. Paris and Leiden: Mouton.

———. 1977. *From Mandeville to Marx: The genesis and triumph of economic ideology*. Chicago: University of Chicago Press.

———. 1980. *Homo hierarchicus: The caste system and its implications*. Chicago: University of Chicago Press.

———. 1982. *On value*. London: The British Academy.

———. 1983. 'The debt to ancestors and the category of *sapinda*'. In Charles Malamoud, ed., *Debt and debtors*, pp. 1–20. New Delhi: Vikas.

Dumont, Louis and David F. Pocock, 1959. 'Pure and impure'. *Contributions to Indian Sociology*, 3: 9–34.

Eliade, Mircea. 1974. *Patterns in comparative religion*. New York: New American Library.

Fortes, Meyer. 1969. *Kinship and social order: The legacy of Lewis Henry Morgan*. Chicago: Aldine Publishing Company.

Fürer-Haimendorf, Christoph von. 1967. *Morals and merit.* London: Weidenfeld and Nicolson.

Gandhi, M. K. 1927. *An autobiography.* English translation by Mahadev Desai. Ahmedabad: Navjivan.

———. 1961. *The way to communal harmony.* Compiled and edited by U. R. Rao. Ahmedabad: Navjivan.

———. 1984. *All men are brothers.* Compiled and edited by Krishna Kripalani. New York: Continuum.

Geertz, Clifford. 1973. *The interpretation of cultures.* New York: Basic Books.

Goffman, Erving. 1961. *Encounters.* New York: Bobbs-Merrill.

Gough, Kathleen. 1981. *Rural society in southeast India.* Cambridge: Cambridge University Press.

Gupta, K. P. 1974. 'Religious evolution and social change in India: A study of the Ramakrishna movement'. *Contributions to Indian Sociology* (n.s.), 8: 25–50.

Heesterman, J. C. 1985. *The inner conflict of tradition: Eassys in Indian ritual, kingship, and society.* Chicago: University of Chicago Press.

Hertz, R. 1960. *Death and the right hand.* Tr. from French by R. and C. Needham. London: Cohen and West.

Hesse, Hermann. 1954. *Siddhartha.* Tr. from German by Hilda Rosner. London: Peter Owen. (Originally published in 1922.)

Hindery, Roderick. 1978. *Comparative ethics in Hindu and Buddhist traditions.* New Delhi: Motilal Banarsidass.

Hiriyana, M. 1949. *The essentials of Indian philosophy.* London: Allen and Unwin.

Inden, Ronald B. and Ralph W. Nicholas. 1977. *Kinship in Bengali culture.* Chicago: University of Chicago Press.

Isherwood, Christopher. 1965. *Ramakrishna and his disciples.* Calcutta: Advaita Ashrama.

Iyer, Raghavan N. 1973. *The moral and political thought of Mahatma Gandhi.* Oxford: Oxford University Press.

Jaini, Padmanabha S. 1979. *The Jaina path of purification.* Delhi: Motilal Banarsidass.

Janakiraman. T. 1972. *The sins of Appu's mother.* Tr. from Tamil by M. Krishnan. Delhi: Orient paperbacks.

Jordens, J. T. F. 1978. *Dayanand Sarasvati: His life and ideas.* Delhi: Oxford University Press.

Joshi, V. C., ed. 1975. *Rammohan Roy and the process of modernization in India.* New Delhi: Vikas Publishing House.

Judah, F. S. 1974. *Hare Krishna and the counter-culture.* New York: John Wiley.

Jung. C. G. 1977. *Memories, dreams, reflections.* London: Fontana Books.

Kachru, Braj B. 1973. *An introduction to spoken Kashmiri.* Part 1 & 2. Urbana: Department of Linguistics, University of Illinois.

Kakar, Sudhir. 1982. *Shamans, mystics and doctors: A psychological inquiry into India and its healing traditions.* Delhi: Oxford University Press.

Kane, Pandurang Vaman. 1941. *History of dharmaśāstra.* Vol. II, Pt. 1. Poona: Bhandarkar Oriental Research Institute.

Kaul, Jayalal. 1973. *Lal Ded*. New Delhi: Sahitya Akademi.

Kellock, James. 1926. *Mahadev Govind Ranade: Patriot and social servant*. Calcutta: Association Press.

Khandekar, Vishnu Sakharam. 1977. *Yayati*. Translated into Hindi from Marathi by Moreshvar Tapasvi. New Delhi: Rajpal.

Khare, R. S. 1976a. *The Hindu hearth and home*. New Delhi: Vikas Publishing House.

———. 1976b. *Culture and reality: Essays on the Hindu system of managing foods*. Simla: Indian Institute of Advanced Study.

Kopf, David. 1979. *The Brahmo Samaj and the shaping of the modern Indian mind*. Princeton: Princeton University Press.

Kothari, R. 1970. *Politics in India*. New Delhi: Orient Longman.

Lakoff, George and Mark Johnson. 1980. *Metaphors we live by*. Chicago: University of Chicago Press.

Langham, Ian. 1981. *The building of British social anthropology*. Dordrecht, Holland: Reidel.

Leach, E. R. 1961. *Pul Eliya, a village in Ceylon: A study of land tenure and kinship*. Cambridge: Cambridge University Press.

Lutyens, Mary, ed. 1970. *The Penguin Krishnamurti reader*. Harmondsworth: Penguin Books.

Madan, T. N. 1965. *Family and kinship: A study of the Pandits of rural Kashmir*. Bombay: Asia Publishing House. (Second edition, 1987, Delhi: Oxford University Press.)

———. 1972. 'Religious ideology in a plural society: The Muslims and Hindus of Kashmir'. *Contributions to Indian Sociology* (n.s.), 6: 106–41.

———. 1975a. 'Structural implications of marriage in north India: Wife-givers and wife-takers among the Pandits of Kashmir'. *Contributions to Indian Sociology* (n.s.), 9, 2: 217–43.

———. 1975b. 'On living intimately with strangers'. In A. Béteille and T. N. Madan, eds., *Encounter and experience: Personal accounts of fieldwork*, pp. 131–6. New Delhi: Vikas Publishing House.

———. 1977. 'The quest for Hinduism'. *International Social Science Journal*, 29, 2: 261–78.

———. 1981a. 'Moral choices: An essay on the unity of asceticism and eroticism'. In A. C. Mayer, ed., *Culture and morality*, pp. 126–52. Delhi: Oxford University Press.

———. 1981b. 'The ideology of the householder among the Pandits of Kashmir'. *Contributions to Indian Sociology*, 15: 223–49. (Reprinted in T. N. Madan, ed., *Way of life: King, householder, renouncer. Essays in honour of Louis Dumont*, pp. 223–49. New Delhi: Vikas Publishing House.)

———. 1983. 'The ideology of the householder among the Kashmiri Pandits'. In Akos Ostor, Lina Fruzzetti and Steve Barnett, eds., *Concepts of person: Kinship, caste and marriage in India*, pp. 99–117, 239–42. Cambridge, Mass.: Harvard University Press.

Malamoud, Charles. 1975. 'Cuire le monde'. *Puruṣārtha*, 1: 91–135.

Malinowski, Bronislaw. 1948. *Magic, science and religion and other essays*. London: Souvenir Press.

Malraux, André. 1968. *Antimemoirs*. Translated from French by Terence Kilmartin. London: Hamish Hamilton.

Marglin, Frédérique Appfel. 1977. 'Power, purity and pollution: Aspects of the caste system reconsidered'. *Contributions to Indian Sociology* (n.s.), 11, 2: 245–70.

———. 1985. *Wives of the god-king: Rituals of the devadasis of Puri*. Delhi: Oxford University Press.

Marriott, McKim. 1977. 'Hindu transactions: Diversity without dualism'. In Bruce Kapferer, ed., *Transactions and meaning: Directions in the anthropology of exchange and symbolic behaviour*. Philadelphia: Institute for the Study of Human Issues.

Marx, Karl. 1853. 'The British rule in India'. *New York Daily Tribune*, 25 June.

Mayne, J. D. 1953. *Treatise on Hindu law and usage*. 11th ed. by N. Chandrasekhara Aiyar. Madras: Higginbothams.

Miller, Barbara Stoler (tr.). 1978. *The hermit and the love thief: Sanskrit poems of Bhartrihari and Bilhaṇa*. New York: Columbia University Press.

———. (ed.). 1984. *Theater of memory: The plays of Kalidasa*. New York: Columbia University Press.

Monier-Williams, M. *A Sanskrit-English dictionary*. 1976. Delhi: Motilal Banarsidass.

Morris, Morris David. 1960. 'Caste and the evolution of industrial workforce in India'. *Proceedings of the American Philosphical Society*, 104, 2: 124–33.

Mukerji, D. P. 1947. *Modern Indian culture*. Bombay: Hind Kitabs.

Murdoch, Iris. 1970. *The sovereignty of good*. London: Routledge and Kegan Paul.

Myrdal, G. 1968. *Asian drama: An inquiry into the poverty of nations*. 3 Vols. New York: Pantheon Books.

Nandy, Ashis. 1980. 'Final encounter. The politics of the assassination of Gandhi'. In Ashis Nandy, *At the edge of psychology*, pp. 70–98. Delhi: Oxford University Press.

———. 1983. *The intimate enemy: Loss and recovery of self under colonialism*. Delhi: Oxford University Press.

Narayanan, Vasudha. 1985. 'On two levels of auspiciousness'. In John Carman and Frédérique Marglin, eds., *Auspiciousness and purity*, pp. 55–64. Leiden: E. J. Brill.

Nehru, J. 1941. *Toward freedom: An autobiography*. New York: Doubleday.

———. 1961. *The discovery of India*. Bombay: Asia Publishing House.

Nikhilananda, Swami. 1953. *Vivekananda*. New York: Ramakrishna-Vivekananda Centre.

O' Flaherty, Wendy Doniger. 1975. *Asceticism and eroticism in the mythology of Śiva*. New Delhi: Oxford University Press.

———. 1976. *The origins of evil in Hindu mythology*. Delhi: Motilal Banarsidass.

Opler, Morris E. 1945. 'Themes as dynamic forces in culture'. *American Journal of Sociology*, 51: 198–206.

Pandey, Raj Bali. 1969. *Hindu saṁskāras: Socio-religious study of the Hindu sacraments*. Delhi: Motilal Banarsidass.

Panikkar, K. M. 1956. *A survey of Indian history*. Bombay: Asia Publishing House.

———. 1963. *The foundations of new India*. London: George Allen and Unwin.

Parry, J. P. 1979. *Caste and kinship in Kangra*. London: Routledge and Kegan Paul.

———. 1981. 'Death and cosmogony in Kashi'. *Contributions to Indian Sociology*, 15: 337–65.

———. 1982. 'Sacrificial death and the necrophagous ascetic'. In Maurice Bloch and Jonathan Parry, eds., *Death and the regeneration of life*, pp. 74–110. Cambridge: Cambridge University Press.

Pelzel, John C. 1974. 'Human nature in the Japanese myths'. In *Japanese culture and behaviour*, ed. T. S. Lebra and W. B. Lebra, pp. 3–26. Honolulu: University Press of Hawaii.

Plath, David W. 1980. *Long engagements*. Stanford: Stanford University Press.

Pocock, D. F. 1973. *Mind, body and wealth: A study of belief and practice in an Indian village*. Oxford: Blackwell Publications.

———. 1976. 'Preservation of the religious life: Hindu immigrants in England'. *Contributions to Indian Sociology* (n.s.), 10: 343–65.

Potter, Karl. 1963. *Presuppositions of India's philosophies*. New Delhi: Prentice-Hall of India.

Putnam, Hilary. 1977. *Meaning and the moral sciences*. London: Routledge and Kegan Paul.

Radhakrishnan, S. 1927. *The Hindu view of life*. London: George Allen and Unwin.

———. 1940. *Eastern religions and Western thought*. London: Oxford University Press. 2nd ed.

———. 1948. *The Bhagavadgītā*. With an introductory essay, Sanskrit text, English translation and notes. London: Allen and Unwin.

———. 1953. *The principal Upaniṣads*. With introduction, translation and notes. London: Allen and Unwin.

Rajagopalachari, C. 1968. *Mahabharata*. Bombay: Bharatiya Vidya Bhawan.

Reeves, P. D. 1971. Introduction in *Sleeman in Oudh: An abridgement of W. H. Sleeman's* A journey through the kingdom of Oude, 1849–1850, pp. 1–40. Cambridge: Cambridge University Press.

Reynolds, Holly Baker. 1980. 'The auspicious married woman'. In *The powers of Tamil women*, ed. Susan S. Wadley, pp. 35–60. Syracuse: Syracuse University.

Sanderson, Alexis. 1985. 'Purity and power among the Brahmans of Kashmir'. In Michael Carrithers et al., eds., *The category of the person*, pp. 190–216. Cambridge: Cambridge University Press.

Saran, A. K. 1963. 'Hinduism and economic development in India'. *Archives de Sociologie des Religions*, 15: 87–94.

———. 1972. 'The two contexts of secularization: Western and Indian'. *Islam and the Modern Age*, 2: 17–32.

Schneider, David M. 1968. *American kinship: A cultural account*. Englewood Cliffs, N.J.: Prentice-Hall.

Schutz, A. 1967. *Collected papers: I. The problems of social reality.* The Hague: Martinus Nijhoff.

———. 1976. *The phenomenology of the social world.* London: Heinemann Educational Books.

Siegel, Lee. 1983. *Fires of love/waters of peace.* Honolulu: University of Hawaii Press.

Singer, M. 1972. *When a great tradition modernizes.* New York: Praeger.

Smith, D. E. 1963. *India as a secular state.* Princeton: Princeton University Press.

Srinivas, M. N. 1942. *Marriage and family in Mysore.* Bombay: New Book Co.

———. 1952. *Religion and society among the Coorgs of south India.* Oxford: Clarendon Press.

———. 1967. 'The cohesive role of sanskritization'. In Philip Mason, ed., *India and Ceylon: Unity and diversity,* pp. 67–82. London: Oxford University Press.

Stevenson, S. 1920. *The rites of the twice-born.* London: Oxford University Press.

Tagore, Rabindranath. 1946. *Gitanjali.* In *Collected poems and plays of Rabindranath Tagore,* pp. 1–48. London: Macmillan.

———. 1955. *Collected poems and plays.* London: Macmillan.

Van Gennep, A. 1960. *The rites of passage.* (English translation by M. B. Vizedom and G. L. Caffee.) Chicago: University of Chicago Press.

Varma, Bhagvaticharan. 1977. *Chitralekha.* (In Hindi.) Allahabad: Bharati Bhandar.

Vas, Luis S. R., ed. 1973. *The mind of J. Krishnamurti.* Bombay: Jaico.

Wadley, S. S. 1975. *Shakti: Power in the conceptual structure of Karimpur religion.* Chicago: University of Chicago Press.

Weber, Max. 1947. *The theory of economic and social organisation.* Glencoe: The Free Press.

———. 1958. *The religion of India.* Tr. from German by H. H. Gerth and D. Martindale. Glencoe: The Free Press.

Wittgenstein, Ludwig. 1964. *The blue and brown books.* Oxford: Basil Blackwell.

Wollheim, Richard. 1984. *The thread of life.* Cambridge, Mass.: Harvard University Press.

Woodroffe, Sir John. 1978. *Shakti and shakta.* 5th ed., 1959. New York: Dover Publications.

Zaehner, R. C. 1962. *Hinduism.* London: Oxford University Press.

INDEX